EXPRESS

Fast, fresh & on the table in under **40 MINUTES**

This edition first published in 2015 by Bounty Books

based on materials licensed to it by Bauer Media Books, Australia. This edition reprinted in 2015.

Bauer Media Books are published by

BAUER MEDIA PTY LIMITED 54 PARK ST, SYDNEY

GPO BOX 4088, SYDNEY, NSW 2001.

phone +61 2 9282 8618; fax +61 2 9126 3702

www.awwcookbooks.com.au

PUBLISHER Jo Runciman
EDITORIAL & FOOD DIRECTOR Pamela Clark
DIRECTOR OF SALES, MARKETING & RIGHTS Brian Cearnes
ART DIRECTOR & DESIGNER Hannah Blackmore
SENIOR EDITOR Wendy Bryant
FOOD EDITOR Sophia Young
OPERATIONS MANAGER David Scotto

Printed by Leo Paper Products in China.

Published and distributed in the United Kingdom by Bounty Books, a division of Octopus Publishing Group Ltd
Carmelite House
50 Victoria Embankment
London, EC4Y 0DZ
United Kingdom
info@octopus-publishing.co.uk;
www.octopusbooks.co.uk

International foreign language rights,
Brian Cearnes, Bauer Media Books
bcearnes@bauer-media.com.au

A catalogue record for this book is available from the British Library.

ISBN: 978-075372-967-0

© Bauer Media Pty Ltd 2015

ABN 18 053 273 546

EXPRESS

Fast, fresh & on the table in under **40 MINUTES**

Bounty Books

Contents

FAST *fresh*

THE DAYS OF THE TRADITIONAL DOMESTIC HOUSEWIFE ARE WELL AND TRULY OVER. WITH MORE MEN AND WOMEN IN THE WORKFORCE, THERE IS LESS TIME TO SPEND PREPARING COMPLEX DISHES IN THE KITCHEN. THIS BOOK PROVES IT'S POSSIBLE TO CREATE DELICIOUS AND NUTRITIOUS MEALS FAST FOR YOU AND YOUR FAMILY.

Fast, no stress

Packed with speedy recipes for breakfasts, mains, snacks and desserts, *Express* is conveniently split into chapters for one and two people, plus recipes for families and guests. You will no longer be forced to cook the same 'quick' meals again and again. Each recipe is tested at least three times in The Australian Women's Weekly Test Kitchen to ensure you get the most out of your limited time.

IN THE SUPERMARKET

With the abundance of supermarket products created for speedy cooking, preparing tasty, wholesome meals has never been so easy. Embrace pre-made sauces, pastes and curries and opt for microwaveable grains, pre-made pizza bases and marinated and diced meats. Look for basic ingredients that can be used in different meals. For example, beef mince can become a taco filling, a hearty meat pie or a classic bolognese sauce. It is common to see peeled, chopped fresh vegetables, mixed salad

leaves and roasted chickens in supermarkets. Make use of convenience products without skimping on health benefits. Ready-cooked rice is nutritionally equal to rice cooked from scratch, so too are ready-made sauces like pesto and hummus. Become familiar with brands that offer the most authentic tastes. Sometimes all you need to transform a meal from bland to brilliant is a simple marinade or dressing. Mix olive oil, garlic and fresh herbs and spices to give any dish a flavour kick with little effort. For best results, leave meat to marinate overnight. Buy a salad from the supermarket and there's dinner on the table.

BUTCHERS & FISHMONGERS

A lot of butchers do a fantastic selection of marinated, trimmed, crumbed, skewered and diced meats, which help cut down on preparation times. If you can't find what you're looking for, ask the butcher to trim and dice the meat so it's ready for cooking. Seafood is a nutritious and healthy meal option, but takes

time to clean, fillet and shell. Most fishmongers are happy to do these jobs for you, and often sell filleted fish, shelled prawns and marinara mixes. Prepared seafood is readily available at most supermarkets.

In the kitchen

Take advantage of kitchen utensils to speed up food preparation. Implementing a good system in the kitchen makes it much easier to work quickly and multi-task. Some of the Test Kitchen's favourite tools include a V-slicer or a mandoline, food processor, blender, sharp knives, scissors, a sharp vegetable peeler and a really sharp grater. Electrical appliances help get the food on the table even faster – microwaves are great for defrosting, cooking potatoes and warming left-overs.

PREPARATION

Ensure the kitchen is always stocked; dedicate one day a week to preparing a realistic weekly menu and shopping list. This way you are not pressed to think of what to cook after a busy and tiring day. Sunday is often a good day for full-time workers to plan next week's menu. For more menu planning ideas, check out *365 Main Meals* and *What Can I Cook Tonight*, two great new cookbooks from The Australian Women's Weekly.

BULK SHOP WEEKLY

Save time by doing a regular bulk shop. Highly perishable items, such as fish, need to be purchased close to the time of cooking, however, it's great to buy large amounts of dry groceries fortnightly or monthly

Stock the pantry

A clean, organised pantry helps you find items quickly. Opened items should be at the front of the cupboard so they are at hand when needed. Mark the date on packets, so you know when it's time to discard them. Aim to have a selection of staples, such as canned beans, tomatoes and tuna on hand. Keep a selection of condiments as these are the flavour builders of a meal – Asian sauces, spices, mustards, vinegars and oils are a must.

pan and saucepan. Utilise the food processor, stick blender and microwave to speed up mixing, grinding and preparation time.

THINK LIKE A CHEF

Professional chefs have a lot to cook in a short space of time, so take a few tips from them. Before picking up a knife, read the recipe from start to finish. This way you know exactly how the recipe flows. It often helps to lay out all the ingredients in the order you need them, slicing and dicing where appropriate. Take out pots, pans

IN SEASON, READILY AVAILABLE FRESH INGREDIENTS ARE GREAT FOR BUDGET CONSCIOUS COOKS.

MEALS WITH KIDS IN MIND – NOT SO SPICY, NOT TOO MUCH CHILLI, BUT STILL FULL OF FLAVOUR.

THIS BUTTON TAKES ALL THE GUESS WORK OUT OF TRYING TO FIND FAST, HEALTHY FOOD CHOICES.

GREAT FOR THOSE NIGHTS YOU CAN'T BE BOTHERED WITH MULTIPLE POTS, PANS AND WASHING UP.

NOT JUST FOR MONDAYS – MEAT-FREE IS A GREAT WAY TO START EATING MORE FRESH VEGIES.

to ensure the pantry is always stocked with commonly used ingredients such as rice, flour and pasta. Keep a chart of seasonal fruit and vegetables handy – this produce is usually available at a cheaper price as it's fresh and plentiful in supply. Make a note on your computer or smart phone of those items you frequently purchase, so you never forget everyday needs. Check the pantry first and compile a grocery list, grouping similar ingredients.

ORGANISE THE KITCHEN

The most important thing when cooking 'fast' is planning ahead. Ensure commonly used utensils are within reach; too much clutter will reduce the amount of bench space available, slow you down and cause chaos in the kitchen. Knives, vegetable peelers and graters should be sharp – blunt blades are dangerous and can be frustrating, especially when you're in a rush. It is essential to have at least one good-quality frying

and other equipment needed for the recipe. Fill the kettle and get it boiling, ready to pour into the pan. Preheat the oven or grill or heat oil in the frying pan.

With practise comes speed

These recipes will help you to quickly prepare a fresh, delicious and nutritious meal. With practise comes speed and confidence in the kitchen, meaning all your favourite recipes can be 'express' recipes in no time at all.

Prep Steps

1 QUICK HERBS

To qyuckly chop soft leaf herbs (flat-leaf parsley, coriander and dill), use your hands to twist off the stems from the bunch in one go, then chop the leaves and e dible stems together.

2 GREAT GRATE

To grate vegetables, such as carrots and zucchini quickly, use the shredder attachment on a food processor, and for cabbage, use the slicer attachment.

3 More juice

To speed and maximise the amount of juice extracted from lemons and limes, first roll the fruit firmly on a hard bench with your hand, or microwave on HIGH (80%) for 15 seconds, before juicing.

4 MARINATING

To make marinating easier, place the marinating ingredients and the meat or fish in a large ziptop bag; seal the bag and massage the marinade into the ingredients. Place it in the fridge for at least 3 hours or overnight.

5 Quick clean

For easy cleaning, and to prevent ingredients sticking to a char-grill pan, line the base of the pan and halfway up the sides with baking paper. Char-grill as instructed in the recipe, then simply toss out the paper when finished.

6 HERB READY

Freeze fresh herbs such as thyme, rosemary and chives, either chopped or in whole-leaf form, in measured quantities in ice-cube trays covered with olive oil. Simply add the herbs straight to your recipe from the freezer.

7 DO AHEAD

Start the recipe the morning or day before. Measure out the ingredients and store the perishable ones in the fridge. Hard vegetables, except potatoes, can be cut on the morning of cooking; store covered with damp paper.

8 Fishy tales

If you aren't a fan of fish skin, there's no need to fuss about trying to remove it before cooking – leave it on, as the skin will hold the delicate flesh of the fish together while it cooks. Peel away the skin when the fish is done.

9 HEAT THE PAN

Most frying pans aren't heavy-based, so heat your pan over medium heat for at least 3 minutes without adding any oil or butter. This way, when the ingredients are added to the pan, it will hold the heat.

10 FOOD PREP

When preparing ingredients, you will save time if you start with the vegetables, then the herbs, and lastly any meat or fish; this way you won't have to wash the chopping board in between preparation.

11 Acidulated water

This is simply water with lemon juice added. Use it to stop fennel, apple and pears from turning brown. Avocado, however, can be stored, cut-side down, in plain water with the skin on to prevent it browning.

12 DON'T PEEL

For carrot, parsnip and sweet potato, simply wash the vegetables and skip peeling. Not only will you save time, you'll also reap the added benefits of all the nutrients found in the vegetable skins. For potato, choose washed varieties.

EXPRESS FOR ONE

YOU CAN USE OTHER TYPES OF NOODLES, SUCH AS RICE OR HOKKIEN. FEEL FREE TO REPLACE THE GREEN BEANS AND CORN WITH OTHER VEGETABLES YOU MIGHT HAVE ON HAND, SUCH AS ASIAN GREENS, BROCCOLI, ASPARAGUS OR CABBAGE. A WOK CHAN IS A SHOVEL-LIKE, FLAT-ENDED IMPLEMENT TRADITIONALLY USED TO MOVE FOOD AROUND A WOK. THE SHAPE MAKES LIFTING AND TURNING EASY. FOR A NON-STICK WOK, CHOOSE A CHAN MADE FROM SILICON; FOR A CARBON STEEL WOK, METAL IS BEST.

Pork and udon NOODLE STIR-FRY

PREP & COOK TIME 20 MINUTES   SERVES 1

1 clove garlic, crushed

1 teaspoon finely grated fresh ginger

1 tablespoon rice cooking wine (shaoxing)

150g (5 ounces) minced (ground) pork

½ teaspoon sesame oil

1 tablespoon kecap manis

2 tablespoons sweet chilli sauce

1 tablespoon vegetable oil

100g (3½ ounces) green beans, trimmed, halved diagonally crossways

60g (2oz) baby corn, halved lengthways

220g (7 ounce) fresh udon noodles

1 green onion (scallion), sliced thinly

1 tablespoon fresh coriander (cilantro) leaves

1 Combine garlic, ginger, cooking wine and pork in a small bowl.

2 Combine sesame oil, kecap manis and sweet chilli sauce in a small jug.

3 Heat vegetable oil in a wok over high heat; stir-fry pork mixture for 5 minutes, breaking up lumps with a chan, or until browned. Add beans and corn; stir-fry for 2 minutes or until vegetables are almost tender.

4 Add sauce mixture and noodles to wok; stir-fry until heated through. Stir in half the green onion. Top with coriander and remaining onion.

tip Fresh udon noodles are available from the refrigerated section of supermarkets. Use your favourite style of fresh noodles, if you prefer.

Cheap
EAT

Healthy
CHOICE

CEVICHE IS A FRESH, TANGY FISH SALAD POPULAR IN LATIN AMERICAN COUNTRIES.
WHILE THE FISH ISN'T COOKED WITH HEAT, THE ACIDITY OF THE LIME JUICE MARINADE
CURES THE FISH, TURNING IT OPAQUE IN THE SAME WAY HEAT WOULD.

Avocado and MANGO CEVICHE

PREP TIME 20 MINUTES (& REFRIGERATION) **SERVES** 1

175g (5½ ounces) skinless firm white fish fillet, chopped finely

2 tablespoons lime juice

¼ small red onion (25g), chopped finely

½ small mango (150g), chopped finely

½ small avocado (100g), chopped finely

½ clove garlic, crushed

¼ teaspoon dried chilli flakes

¼ cup fresh coriander leaves (cilantro)

½ baby cos (romaine) lettuce, leaves separated

1 Combine fish and lime juice in a medium bowl. Cover; refrigerate for 15 minutes. Drain fish; add onion, mango, avocado, garlic, chilli and coriander, stir to combine. Season to taste.

2 Serve ceviche with lettuce leaves and accompany with toasted seeded bread, if you like.

tips Use extremely fresh sashimi-grade white-fleshed fish, or salmon or tuna for this dish. Raw fish sold as sashimi has to meet stringent guidelines regarding its handling and treatment after leaving the water. We suggest you seek local advice from authorities before eating any raw seafood. The recipe can easily be doubled for two or expanded for a family. You could also serve the ceviche in soft warmed corn tortillas.

TRY PORK AND FENNEL SAUSAGES OR EVEN A SPICY SAUSAGE, LIKE FRESH CHORIZO OR MERGUEZ, FOR ADDED FLAVOUR. IMPROVISE, IF YOU LIKE, WITH WHAT YOU HAVE ON HAND. YOU CAN SWAP ROCKET OR KALE FOR SPINACH, AND SWISS BROWN OR PORTOBELLO FOR THE FLAT MUSHROOMS, WHILE THE BREAD CAN BE ANY SORT.

Egg and
SAUSAGE BAKE

PREP & COOK TIME 20 MINUTES SERVES 1

2 pork sausages (240g)

20g (¾ ounces) butter

2 large flat mushrooms (160g), chopped coarsely

80g (2½ ounces) baby spinach leaves

6 cherry tomatoes, halved

1 egg

1 slice sourdough bread, torn into chunks

2 tablespoons finely grated parmesan

2 tablespoons fresh flat-leafed parsley leaves

1 Preheat oven to 200°C/400°F.

2 Cook sausages in a small ovenproof frying pan, over medium heat, for 6 minutes or until just cooked; remove from pan. Cut each sausage in half horizontally.

3 Add butter and mushroom to same pan; cook, stirring, for 1 minute or until tender. Add three-quarters of the spinach; stir until just wilted.

4 Return sausage to pan; add tomato, then carefully break egg on top of tomato. Season and top with bread.

5 Bake in oven for 8 minutes or until the egg white is set, the yolk still runny, and the bread is browned. Top with remaining spinach, parmesan and parsley.

Cheap
EAT

Meat FREE

THE AMOUNT OF FILLING LOOKS LIKE QUITE A LOT, HOWEVER, KEEP IN MIND THAT THE SPINACH WILL COLLAPSE DURING COOKING. DOUBLE THE RECIPE AND REHEAT THE PIE FOR LUNCH THE NEXT DAY IN A MICROWAVE.

Greek spinach AND FETTA PIE

PREP & COOK TIME 30 MINUTES SERVES 1

½ cup (120g) firm fresh ricotta

50g (1½ ounces) fetta, crumbled

1 teaspoon dried oregano

1 green onion (scallion), sliced thinly

1 tablespoon finely chopped pitted kalamata olives

40g (1 ounce) baby spinach leaves, sliced thinly

¼ cup coarsely chopped fresh dill

1 egg, beaten lightly

1 sheet puff pastry

¼ cup (70g) greek-style yoghurt

1 small clove garlic, crushed

green salad, to serve

1 Preheat oven to 220°C/425°F. Line an oven tray with baking paper.

2 Combine cheeses, oregano, onion, olives, spinach and 2 tablespoons of dill in a small bowl; add all but 1 teaspoon of the beaten egg and mix well. Season with freshly ground black pepper. (Reserve remaining egg to brush pastry).

3 Using a 24cm (9½-inch) plate or bowl as a guide, cut out a circle from the pastry. Spoon ricotta mixture over one half of the pastry, leaving a 2cm (¾-inch) border. Brush border with reserved beaten egg; fold pastry over to enclose filling; press edge to seal. Brush top with remaining beaten egg.

4 Place pie on tray; bake for 20 minutes or until pastry is browned.

5 Meanwhile, combine remaining dill, yoghurt and garlic in a small bowl. Serve pie with dill yoghurt and a green salad.

do-ahead Uncooked pie can be prepared several hours ahead. Store covered, in the fridge.

SHALLOTS ARE A SMALL, MILDER-TASTING MEMBER OF THE ONION FAMILY. THE SIZE MAKES THEM PERFECT FOR SOLO DINNERS, PLUS THEY WILL STORE FOR MONTHS IF KEPT IN A BASKET AT ROOM TEMPERATURE. HOWEVER, YOU COULD ALSO USE A GREEN ONION.

Blt salad
WITH SMOKY CHICKEN

PREP & COOK TIME 20 MINUTES SERVES 1

2 rindless bacon slices (130g)

½ teaspoon smoked paprika

2 teaspoons olive oil

3 chicken tenderloins (225g)

½ teaspoon dijon mustard

2 teaspoons lemon juice

2 teaspoons water

2 tablespoons greek-style yoghurt

1 small clove garlic, crushed

1 shallot (25g), sliced finely

1 baby (romaine) cos lettuce, trimmed, leaves separated

4 cherry or grape tomatoes, halved

1 tablespoon fresh flat-leaf parsley leaves

1 Cook bacon in a medium frying pan, over medium heat, for 3 minutes or until crisp; drain on paper towel, then tear into large pieces.

2 Combine paprika, oil and chicken in a small bowl. Season.

3 Add chicken to same pan; cook for 2 minutes each side or until cooked through. Shred chicken coarsely.

4 Stir mustard, juice, water, yoghurt and garlic in a small bowl or jug.

5 Layer shallot, lettuce, tomato, chicken and bacon in a shallow bowl; drizzle with yoghurt dressing.

do-ahead Yoghurt dressing can be prepared several hours ahead; store, covered, in the fridge.

tip Use basil instead of parsley leaves, if you like.

Grilled prawns with
AVOCADO CREAM AND SLAW

Grilled prawns with AVOCADO CREAM AND SLAW

AVOCADO CREAM AND SLAW

PREP & COOK TIME 20 MINUTES SERVES 1

12 uncooked small king prawns (shrimp) (420g)

1 teaspoon piri piri seasoning

2 teaspoons olive oil

½ small ripe avocado (100g)

1 tablespoon lime juice

1 tablespoon cold water

1 cup (80g) finely shredded cabbage

1 small carrot (70g), cut into matchsticks

1 green onion (scallion), sliced thinly

1 teaspoon extra virgin olive oil

2 tablespoons fresh coriander leaves (cilantro), torn

lime wedges, to serve

1 Shell and devein prawns leaving tails intact. Combine prawns, seasoning and olive oil in a small bowl.

2 Mash avocado, juice and water in a small bowl using a fork until mixture is coarsely mixed.

3 Combine cabbage, carrot, onion and extra virgin olive oil in a medium bowl; season to taste.

4 Cook prawns on a heated oiled grill pan or frying pan for 1 minute each side or until cooked through.

5 Serve prawns with avocado cream and cabbage salad; top with coriander leaves and accompany with lime wedges.

tips For speed, use a mandoline or V-slicer to cut the carrot, or the coarse holes on a box grater. You can use an Asian vegetable peeler to peel the carrot into long thin strands. These are sold at Asian grocers and select kitchen shops.

IF YOU EAT LOTS OF LENTILS, CONSIDER COOKING A LARGE BATCH OF DRIED LENTILS AHEAD OF TIME TO SAVE MONEY AND TO DECREASE YOUR SODIUM INTAKE (CANNED LENTILS TEND TO HAVE A HIGH SODIUM CONTENT). SMALL GREEN LENTILS WILL TAKE 20 MINUTES TO COOK FROM BOILING, WHILE BROWN OR LARGE GREEN LENTILS WILL TAKE 30 MINUTES. ONCE COOKED, DRAIN, THEN TOSS WITH A LITTLE OLIVE OIL. COOL, THEN PORTION INTO SMALL FREEZER BAGS. DEFROST IN THE FRIDGE BEFORE USING.

Lentil, green bean
AND FETTA SALAD

PREP & COOK TIME 12 MINUTES   SERVES 1

125g (4 ounces) green beans, trimmed, halved diagonally

2 large cherry tomatoes (25g), quartered

⅔ cup (110g) canned brown lentils, rinsed, drained

½ cup baby rocket leaves (arugula)

1 teaspoon dijon mustard

½ teaspoon honey

1½ tablespoons lemon juice

2 tablespoons extra virgin olive oil

50g (1½ ounces) persian fetta, crumbled

1 Boil, steam or microwave beans until tender; drain.

2 Place beans, tomato, lentils and rocket in a serving bowl.

3 Whisk mustard, honey, juice and oil in a small bowl; season to taste.

4 Add dressing to salad; toss gently to combine. Sprinkle with fetta to serve.

Meat
FREE

TRY OTHER VEGETABLES IN THE KUMARA FILLING, SUCH AS CHOPPED SPINACH, PEAS, CORN OR GREEN BEANS. STARTING THE COOKING PROCESS OF THE KUMARA IN THE MICROWAVE REDUCES THE COOKING TIME BY MORE THAN HALF. HOWEVER, IF YOU DON'T HAVE A MICROWAVE, YOU CAN DO STEP 2 IN THE OVEN. WRAP KUMARA IN FOIL, ROAST AT 200°C/400°F FOR 40 MINUTES; UNWRAP AND PROCEED WITH THE RECIPE.

Broccoli and walnut STUFFED SWEET POTATO

PREP & COOK TIME 30 MINUTES SERVES 1

1 medium kumara (orange sweet potato) (400g)

60g (2 ounces) broccoli, chopped finely

¼ cup (25g) crumbed walnuts

2 tablespoons finely chopped fresh chives

3 teaspoons wholegrain mustard

⅓ cup (40g) grated vintage cheddar

1 egg

1 Preheat oven to 220°C/425°F.

2 Prick kumara all over with a sharp knife. Microwave on HIGH (100%) for 10 minutes or until soft.

3 When cool enough to handle, trim top off kumara; scoop flesh into a small bowl and mash. Stir in broccoli, walnuts, 1½ tablespoons of the chives, mustard and ¼ cup of the cheddar Season to taste.

4 Spoon broccoli mixture into kumara. Place kumara on a baking-paper-lined oven tray; sprinkle with remaining cheddar. Bake for 10 minutes or until golden.

5 Meanwhile, fry egg in a heated, oiled small frying pan for 2 minutes or until cooked as desired; season. Top kumara with egg; sprinkle over remaining chives.

tip Crumbed walnuts, so labelled, are available in the baking aisle at most supermarkets; if you can't find them, simply coarsely chop whole walnuts.

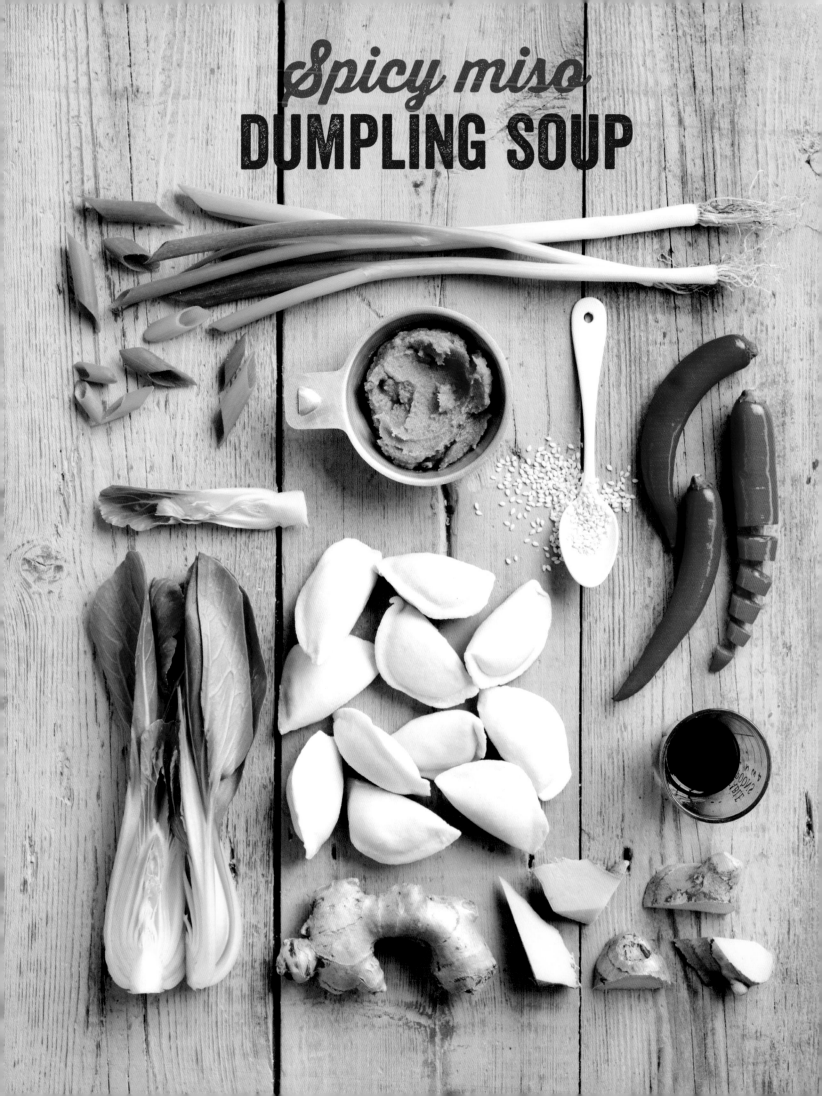

Spicy miso DUMPLING SOUP

SHIRO (WHITE) MISO IS AVAILABLE FROM SUPERMARKETS AND WILL KEEP FOR MONTHS STORED IN THE FRIDGE. USE IT AS A SEASONING IN STIR-FRIES OR SOUPS.

Spicy miso DUMPLING SOUP

PREP & COOK TIME 15 MINUTES   SERVES 1

1½ cups (375ml) water

1 tablespoon shiro miso paste

½ fresh long red chilli, sliced thinly

½ teaspoon finely grated fresh ginger

1 teaspoon light soy sauce

5 frozen pork dumplings

1 baby buk choy (150g), quartered

½ green onion (scallion), sliced thinly diagonally

½ teaspoon sesame seeds, toasted

1 Place water, miso, chilli, ginger and sauce in a small saucepan over medium heat; bring to a simmer, stirring occasionally, until well combined.

2 Add dumplings, cook for 6 minutes or until heated through. Add buk choy, cook for a further 2 minutes. Spoon into a bowl; serve topped with green onion and sesame seeds.

tip You can use vegetarian or chicken dumplings instead of the pork.

Teriyaki beef
WITH PICKLED CABBAGE

WITH PICKLED CABBAGE

PREP & COOK TIME 20 MINUTES SERVES 1

80g (2½ ounces) red cabbage, sliced thinly

2 tablespoons rice wine vinegar

½ clove garlic, crushed

½ teaspoon finely grated fresh ginger

1 teaspoon caster (superfine) sugar

200g (6½ ounce) scotch fillet steak, trimmed

2 tablespoons teriyaki sauce

2 teaspoons vegetable oil

½ x 250g (8-ounce) packet 90-second microwave brown rice

2 teaspoons teriyaki sauce, extra

2 tablespoons fresh coriander leaves (cilantro)

1 Combine cabbage, vinegar, garlic, ginger and sugar in a medium bowl; season. Stand for 5 minutes for cabbage to pickle.

2 Combine steak, sauce and oil in a small bowl. Cook steak in a heated oiled frying pan, for 2 minutes each side for medium, or until cooked as desired. Rest, loosely covered with foil, for 5 minutes before slicing.

3 Heat rice according to packet directions. Drain cabbage from marinade. Serve cabbage with rice and steak. Drizzle with extra sauce; sprinkle with coriander before serving.

tip You can also use white rice.

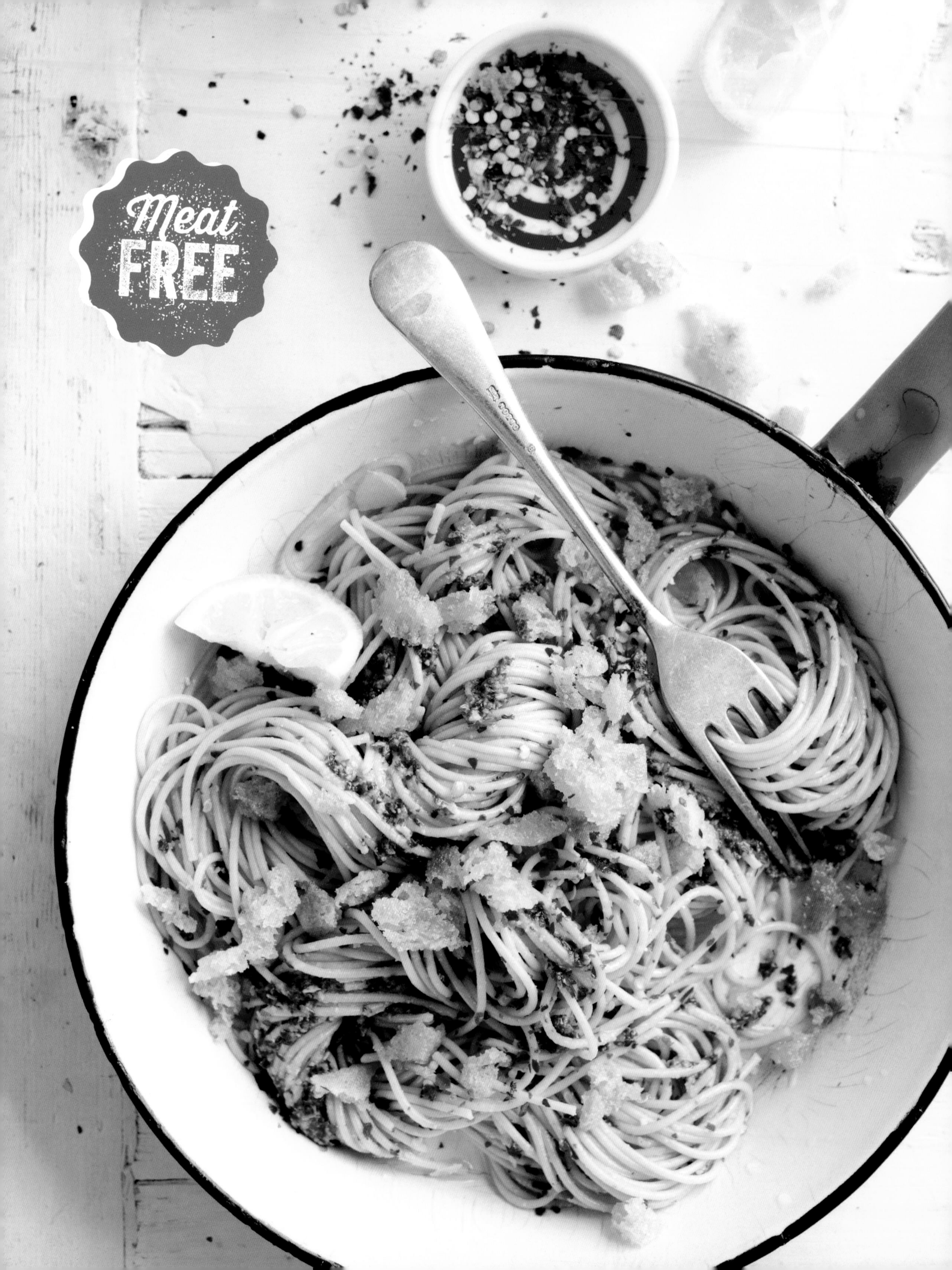
Meat
FREE

THIS IS A GREAT WAY TO USE UP LEAFY GREENS AND HERBS. FOR THE PESTO, TRY SUBSTITUTING BASIL OR MINT FOR THE PARSLEY, AND ROCKET OR BABY SPINACH FOR THE KALE. YOU COULD ALSO USE BABY KALE THAT IS SOLD IN PACKETS FROM THE SUPERMARKET.

Kale, chilli and PARMESAN PASTA

PREP & COOK TIME 20 MINUTES   SERVES 1

½ cup (15g) curly kale, torn coarsely

½ cup (30g) parmesan, grated finely

¼ cup firmly packed fresh flat-leaf parsley

1 small garlic clove, crushed

1 teaspoon finely grated lemon rind

2 tablespoons lemon juice

¼ cup (60ml) extra virgin olive oil, plus extra for drizzling

⅓ cup (40g) sourdough, torn coarsely

125g (4 ounces) spelt or wholemeal spaghettini

pinch dried chilli flakes

1 To make kale pesto, process kale, parmesan, parsley, garlic, rind, half the juice and 2 tablespoons of the oil in a small food processor; season to taste.

2 Heat remaining oil in a small frying pan over medium-high heat; add sourdough, stir for 2 minutes or until lightly golden. Transfer to a plate lined with paper towel.

3 Cook pasta in a large saucepan of boiling water until almost tender. Reserve 2 tablespoons of the cooking water then drain pasta. Return pasta to pan with reserved cooking water; stir in kale pesto and remaining juice. Season to taste.

4 Serve pasta topped with toasted sourdough, chilli flakes, and extra parmesan, if you like.

Lemon grass and CHICKEN BANH MI BOWL

PREP & COOK TIME 25 MINUTES SERVES 1

2 small chicken thigh fillets (200g)

3 teaspoons lemon grass paste

¼ teaspoon dried chilli flakes

2 teaspoons vegetable oil

1 small carrot (70g), sliced thinly

70g (2½ ounces) daikon, sliced thinly

2 tablespoons white wine vinegar

1 teaspoon caster (superfine) sugar

½ x 250g (8-ounce) packet 90-second microwave white rice

2 teaspoons light soy sauce

1 green onion (scallion), sliced thinly

½ lebanese cucumber (65g), sliced thinly

2 tablespoons fresh coriander leaves (cilantro)

1½ tablespoons mayonnaise

3 teaspoons sriracha chilli sauce

1 lime wedge

1 Combine chicken, lemon grass, chilli and oil in a small bowl, season; stand for 5 minutes.

2 Meanwhile, combine carrot, daikon, vinegar and sugar in a medium bowl, season; stand for 5 minutes. Drain.

3 Cook chicken on a heated oiled grill plate (or grill or barbecue) for 3 minutes each side or until cooked through. Cut chicken thickly widthways.

4 Heat rice following manufacturer's instructions; place in a bowl, drizzle with soy sauce; top with chicken, pickled vegetables, green onion, cucumber and coriander.

5 Combine mayonnaise and chilli sauce. Serve with chicken and lime wedge.

tips For a vegetarian option, substitute firm tofu for chicken. Sriracha is a thai-style chilli sauce available from selected supermarkets and Asian food stores. Substitute with whatever chilli sauce you have on hand, or use a little fresh seeded chilli. Lemon grass paste is available from the fresh food aisle of major supermarkets.

Healthy
CHOICE

Food processor
GRATED SALADS

Moroccan
VEGETABLE SALAD

PREP TIME 20 MINUTES **SERVES** 4

Using the shredder attachment on a food processor, grate 2 raw, peeled medium beetroot, 1 bunch red radish, 2 medium zucchini and 1 large carrot; tip vegetables onto a platter. Wipe food processor bowl clean. Process ⅓ cup extra virgin olive oil, 2 tablespoons pomegranate molasses, 2 tablespoons lemon juice, ½ teaspoon each ground cumin, sumac and salt until combined. Drizzle half the dressing over the vegetables. Rinse and drain 400g (12½oz) canned chickpeas; combine with remaining dressing and 250g (8oz) halved cherry tomatoes in a medium bowl. Top salad with chickpea mixture, sprinkle with ½ cup lightly packed fresh mint. Serve with 1½ cups pitta crisps.

Salad of
CRUNCHY THINGS

PREP & COOK TIME 20 MINUTES **SERVES** 4

Stir 1 tablespoon olive oil and 2 tablespoons each sesame seeds, sunflower seeds and pepitas in a small frying pan, over medium heat, for 5 minutes or until golden. Add 2 teaspoons chia seeds and 1 tablespoon tamari; stir to combine. Using the shredder attachment on a food processor, grate 2 medium kohlrabi and 400g (12½oz) brussels sprouts. Tip vegetables into a large bowl. Process 4 purple kale leaves until chopped coarsely; add to bowl with ¾ cup loosely packed fresh flat-leaf parsley leaves. Process ¼ cup extra virgin olive oil, 2 tablespoons lemon juice, 1 clove crushed garlic and 2 teaspoons dijon mustard; season. Toss vegetables with dressing; top with seed mixture.

Vietnamese CHICKEN SALAD

PREP TIME 30 MINUTES **SERVES** 4

Using the shredder attachment on a food processor, grate 200g (6½oz) white cabbage; transfer to a small bowl. Grate 1 large carrot; tip into a large bowl, add 1 thinly sliced medium red onion, ½ cup rice wine vinegar, 2 teaspoons salt and 2 tablespoons caster (superfine) sugar; stand for 5 minutes. Add 1½ cups bean sprouts; stand for 3 minutes. Drain pickled vegetables; return to the bowl. Add cabbage, 500g (1lb) shredded barbecue chicken, ⅓ cup each fresh mint and coriander (cilantro) leaves. Place ¼ cup water, 1 clove crushed garlic, 2 tablespoons each fish sauce, caster sugar and lime juice in a screw-top jar; shake well. Pour dressing over salad; toss to combine. Sprinkle salad with 2 tablespoons each crushed roasted salted cashews and fried shallots.

Red SALAD

PREP TIME 30 MINUTES **SERVES** 4

Using the slicer attachment on a food processor, slice 1 medium red onion and ½ medium red cabbage. Whisk ⅔ cup white wine vinegar and ¼ cup caster (superfine) sugar in a large bowl until sugar dissolves. Add cabbage mixture; stand for 20 minutes. Drain and discard excess dressing from bowl; season vegetable mixture to taste. Cut 250g (8oz) pre-cooked beetroot into wedges. Cut 2 small radicchio into thin wedges; arrange on a platter with beetroot and cabbage mixture. Crumble over 150g (4½oz) soft goat's cheese; top with ¼ cup each coarsely chopped dry-roasted almonds and chives. Drizzle with 1 tablespoon extra virgin olive oil.

Soy-glazed OCEAN TROUT WITH GREENS

PREP & COOK TIME 25 MINUTES   SERVES 1

¼ cup (60ml) soy sauce

2 tablespoons caster (superfine) sugar

2 teaspoons finely grated fresh ginger

1 teaspoon sesame oil

2 tablespoons rice wine vinegar

200g (6½-ounce) boneless ocean trout fillet

2 stems choy sum (55g), chopped coarsely

½ cup (50g) sugar snap peas

¼ cup (40g) frozen peas, thawed

2 tablespoons fresh coriander (cilantro), chopped coarsely

2 green onions (scallions), sliced thinly diagonally

toasted sesame seeds, extra coriander and steamed brown rice, to serve (optional)

1 Preheat oven to 220°C/425°F.

2 Combine sauce, sugar, ginger, oil and half the vinegar in a small saucepan; cook marinade, over high heat, for 4 minutes or until thickened.

3 Place trout on a small baking-paper-lined oven tray; brush half the marinade over trout. Roast, in oven, for 8 minutes or until golden and almost cooked through.

4 Meanwhile, bring a large saucepan of salted water to the boil. Add choy sum, cook for 1 minute; add sugar snap peas and peas, cook for a further minute or until vegetables are tender crisp. Drain well; transfer to a serving bowl with coriander and onion.

5 Flake trout, discarding skin, add to bowl with remaining marinade and vinegar; toss gently to combine.

6 Top with sesame seeds and extra coriander, and serve with rice, if you like.

TO SPEED PREPARATION, GET THE CARROTS INTO THE OVEN FIRST AND WHILE THEY ARE COOKING, PICK THE HERBS. YOU COULD MAKE A DOUBLE QUANTITY OF THIS SALAD AND TAKE THE OTHER HALF TO LUNCH THE FOLLOWING DAY.

Roasted chickpea and CARROT SALAD WITH FETTA

PREP & COOK TIME 30 MINUTES SERVES 1

1 bunch baby (dutch) carrots (185g), trimmed

400g (12½ ounces) canned chickpeas, rinsed, drained

2 tablespoons extra virgin olive oil

1 teaspoon finely grated lemon rind

1½ teaspoons each cumin, coriander and fennel seeds, crushed lightly

½ cup each loosely packed fresh mint and flat-leaf parsley

¼ cup loosely packed fresh dill sprigs

2 tablespoons lemon juice

100g (3 ounces) drained marinated fetta, plus 1 tablespoon of the marinating oil

crusty bread, to serve

1 Preheat oven to 220°C/425°F.

2 Combine carrots, chickpeas, oil, rind and seeds on a baking-paper-lined oven tray; season. Roast in oven for 25 minutes or until carrots are golden and tender. Transfer to a serving bowl.

3 Combine herbs in a small bowl; drizzle with juice, season to taste. Sprinkle herbs over carrot and chickpea mixture. Top with fetta, then drizzle with a little of the marinating oil. Accompany with crusty bread, if you like.

IF YOUR FRYING PAN IS A FEW CENTIMETRES SMALLER OR LARGER DON'T BE CONCERNED, SIMPLY ADJUST THE COOKING TIME SLIGHTLY TO COMPENSATE FOR THE DIFFERENT THICKNESS OF THE PANCAKE. IF THE HANDLE OF THE FRYING PAN IS NOT OVENPROOF, WRAP IT IN FOIL.

Prawn & veg JAPANESE PANCAKE

PREP & COOK TIME 25 MINUTES SERVES 1

If you can't eat all of this crazy pancake for dinner, it makes a great lunch the next day.

1 tablespoon tomato sauce (ketchup)

2½ teaspoons worcestershire sauce

1½ teaspoons oyster sauce

1 teaspoon caster (superfine) sugar

¼ cup (35g) plain (all-purpose) flour

¼ cup (60ml) water

1 egg

4 uncooked prawns (60g), shelled, chopped coarsely

1 small zucchini (90g), grated coarsely

1 baby carrot (20g), grated coarsely

1 cup (60g) cabbage, sliced thinly

3 green onions (scallions), sliced thinly

2 teaspoons vegetable oil

2 slices streaky bacon (60g), trimmed to fit pan

japanese-style mayonnaise (kewpie) and lemon wedge, to serve

1 Preheat grill to high heat.

2 Whisk sauces and sugar in a small bowl.

3 Whisk flour, water and egg in a medium bowl until smooth. Add prawns, zucchini, carrot, half the cabbage and half the onion; season.

4 Heat oil in a 16cm (6½-inch) ovenproof frying pan over medium-high heat. Add pancake mixture; spread evenly in pan. Cook for 4 minutes or until golden on the base. Place bacon over the top; transfer to the grill. Cook for 8 minutes or until golden and cooked through.

5 Slide pancake onto a plate. Drizzle with sauce mixture and mayonnaise; sprinkle with remaining onion and cabbage; serve with a lemon wedge.

tip Japanese pancakes, or okonomiyaki as they are also known – meaning 'what you like', are customised using toppings for texture and flavour. To our pancake you could add prepared fried noodles and shredded nori, or even pickled pink ginger.

Spiced steak with GRILLED EGGPLANT SALAD

PREP & COOK TIME 15 MINUTES   SERVES 1

2 tablespoons extra virgin olive oil

1 teaspoon ground allspice

1 lebanese eggplant (100g), halved lengthwise

200g (6½ ounces) beef scotch steak

1 small tomato (90g), chopped roughly

1 green onion (scallion), sliced thinly

¼ cup fresh mint leaves

2 teaspoons pomegranate molasses

1 Heat a grill pan over medium-high heat. Place 1 tablespoon of the oil and the allspice in a medium bowl; season with salt and freshly ground black pepper. Toss eggplant in mixture to coat; shake off excess. Toss steak in mixture to coat.

2 Cook steak for 2 minutes each side for medium-rare or until cooked to your liking. Remove, cover loosely with foil; rest for 5 minutes. Add eggplant to same pan; cook for 2 minutes each side or until softened.

3 Meanwhile, place tomato, green onion and mint on a plate. Whisk remaining oil and pomegranate molasses in a small bowl until combined; season to taste.

4 Slice steak and eggplant and transfer plate. Drizzle with pomegranate dressing to serve.

tips Accompany with couscous or flatbread, to serve, if you like. You can use a lamb backstrap in place of the beef.

THIS DELICIOUS AND HEALTHY PAIRING OF FISH WITH TAHINI YOGHURT

IS A POPULAR COMBINATION THROUGHOUT THE MIDDLE EAST.

Steamed fish WITH TAHINI YOGHURT

PREP & COOK TIME 25 MINUTES SERVES 1

200g (6½ ounces) skinless barramundi fillet or other firm white fish

2 tablespoons lemon juice

1 small zucchini (90g), trimmed, sliced lengthways into ribbons

2 red radishes (70g), trimmed, sliced thinly

1 teaspoon tahini (sesame seed paste)

1 tablespoon greek-style yoghurt

1½ tablespoons finely chopped fresh coriander (cilantro)

2 tablespoons toasted slivered almonds

¼ teaspoon dried chilli flakes

1 tablespoon extra virgin olive oil

1 tablespoon fresh coriander (cilantro) leaves, extra

1 Place fish in a steamer lined with baking paper. Place steamer over a saucepan of simmering water. Cook, covered, for 8 minutes or until just cooked through.

2 Meanwhile, combine juice, zucchini and radish in a small bowl; stand until vegetables are pickled, or until needed.

3 Combine tahini and yoghurt in a small bowl; season. Combine coriander, nuts, chilli and half the oil in another small bowl.

4 Carefully transfer fish from steamer to a plate. Cover generously with tahini yoghurt mixture, then top with coriander mixture.

5 Add remaining oil to bowl with zucchini and radish, season; toss to combine.

6 Serve fish with pickled vegetables; accompany with couscous or flatbread, if you like.

tips You could make the recipe using ocean trout or salmon, if you like. Replace the zucchini with a shaved bulb of baby fennel. Use a mandoline or V-slicer to thinly slice the radish and zucchini.

Healthy CHOICE

Healthy CHOICE

SERVE WITH STEAMED BASMATI RICE OR FLATBREAD AND LIME WEDGES.
THE RECIPE MAKES ENOUGH FOR TWO MEALS; COOL HALF THE MIXTURE,
THEN REFRIGERATE IN AN AIRTIGHT CONTAINER.

Lamb and CAULIFLOWER CURRY

PREP & COOK TIME 20 MINUTES SERVES 1

½ small cauliflower (500g), cut into florets

2 tablespoons ghee or vegetable oil

400g (12½ ounces) lamb tenderloins, cut into 2cm (¾-inch) pieces

3 teaspoons garam masala

1 teaspoon ground turmeric

1 small red onion, grated coarsely

2 cloves garlic, crushed

250g (8 ounces) cherry tomatoes

1 tablespoon small fresh mint leaves

1 lime, cut into wedges

mint yoghurt

½ cup (140g) greek-style yoghurt

2 tablespoons coarsely chopped fresh mint

1½ tablespoons lime juice

1 Cook cauliflower in a medium saucepan of boiling water for 4 minutes or until almost tender. Drain; refresh under cold running water.

2 Meanwhile, heat half the ghee in a large saucepan over high heat. Cook lamb for 2 minutes until browned; season with salt, remove from pan.

3 Reduce heat to medium. Add remaining ghee, spices, onion, garlic and tomatoes to pan; cook, stirring, for 5 minutes or until onion has softened.

4 Return lamb and cauliflower to pan; stir to combine. Cook for 2 minutes or until heated through.

5 Meanwhile, make mint yoghurt.

6 Top curry with mint leaves; serve with yoghurt and wedges.

mint yoghurt Combine yoghurt, mint and juice in a small bowl. Season with salt.

ANY ALL-ROUNDER POTATO VARIETY, SUCH AS SEBAGO OR SPUNTA, CAN BE USED INSTEAD OF DESIREE POTATOES. YOU COULD USE 2 RASHERS OF BACON IN PLACE OF THE CHICKEN.

Potato wedges and CHICKEN POUTINE

PREP & COOK TIME 30 MINUTES SERVES 1

Poutine is a Canadian comfort food consisting of chips, gravy and melted cheese, which has morphed to sometimes include chicken or minced beef.

2 desiree potatoes (400g)

¼ barbecue chicken (300g)

20g (¾ ounce) butter

1½ tablespoons plain (all-purpose) flour

1 large shallot, sliced thinly

1 cup (250ml) salt-reduced chicken stock

¼ cup (60ml) vegetable oil

50g (1½ ounces) mozzarella, grated

1 tablespoon coarsely chopped fresh flat-leaf parsley

1 Prick potatoes all over with a fork; microwave on HIGH (100%) for 5 minutes or until tender. When cool enough to handle, cut each potato into six wedges.

2 Meanwhile, shred chicken and skin, reserving bones.

3 To make gravy, melt butter in a small saucepan over medium heat. Once foaming, add flour; cook, stirring, for 1 minute or until dry and golden. Add shallot and chicken bones; stir a further 2 minutes or until shallot softens. Increase heat to medium-high. Gradually stir in stock; cook, stirring, for 4 minutes or until thickened and reduced by a quarter. Remove and discard bones; season to taste. Cover gravy to keep warm.

4 Meanwhile, preheat grill to high. Heat a small ovenproof frying pan over medium-high heat. Cook potato, turning occasionally, for 6 minutes or until golden. Drain off excess oil. Top potato with chicken; sprinkle with mozzarella, heat under grill for 4 minutes or until mozzarella melts and chicken is warmed through. Pour gravy over top; sprinkle with parsley to serve.

Chilli and
CHICKEN TOSTADA

Healthy CHOICE

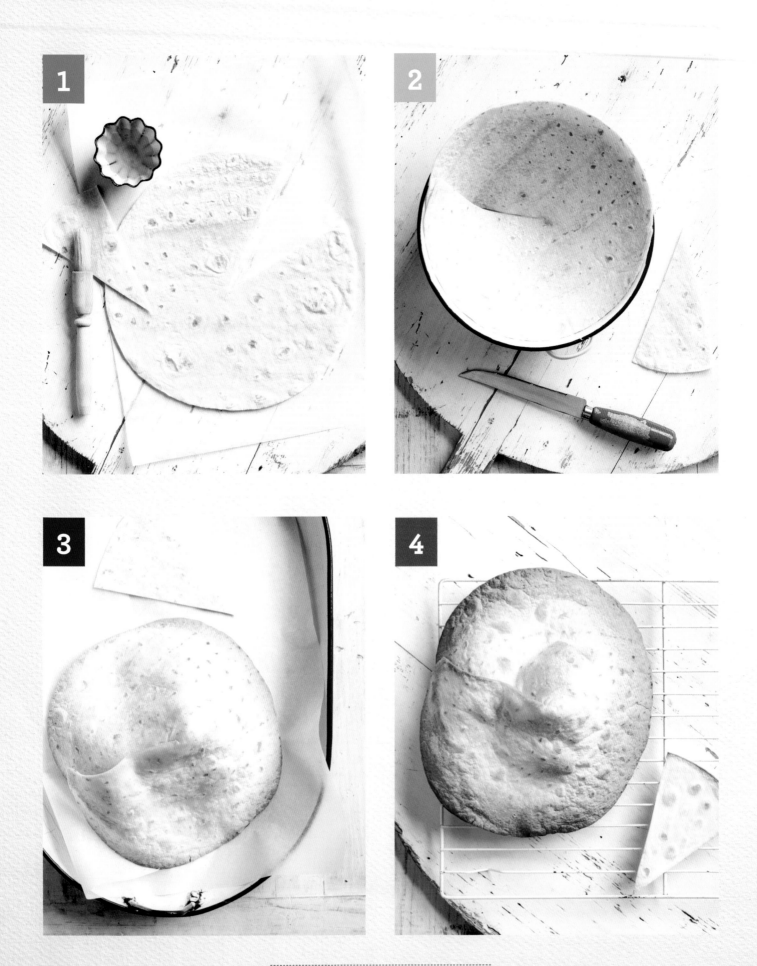

Chilli and CHICKEN TOSTADA

PREP & COOK TIME 25 MINUTES SERVES 1

The recipe can easily be doubled for two people. For a vegetarian tostada, replace the chicken in step 3 with a 400g (12½ ounces) can of rinsed, drained kidney beans.

1 jumbo tortilla or wrap

1 tablespoon vegetable oil, plus extra for brushing

1½ tablespoons finely chopped chipotle chilli in adobo sauce

2 chicken thigh fillets (400g), trimmed

½ corn cob (400g)

2 large cherry tomatoes (25g), seeded, diced finely

1 lime, quartered

1 tablespoon finely chopped fresh coriander (cilantro)

½ x 250g (8 ounce) packet 90-second microwave brown rice

2 tablespoons coriander (cilantro) sprigs

½ cup (40g) thinly sliced red cabbage

1 tablespoon sour cream

1 Preheat oven to 180°C/350°F.

2 Cut an 8cm (3¼-inch) wedge from tortilla. Brush tortilla and wedge on both sides with oil. Place tortilla in an ovenproof bowl, slightly overlapping the cut edge to form the shape of a bowl. Bake in oven for 6 minutes. Carefully transfer tortilla, domed side up, to a small oven tray with the tortilla wedge; bake for a further 6 minutes or until golden. The tortilla bowl (tostada) and tortilla wedge will crisp as they cool.

3 Meanwhile, combine half the chilli and oil in a small bowl; season with salt. Add chicken; turn to coat in mixture.

4 Heat a frying pan over high heat. Cook chicken for 4 minutes each side or until cooked through, adding corn to the pan during the last 4 minutes. Rest chicken for 5 minutes, then thinly slice chicken and corn kernels from cob.

5 Meanwhile, combine remaining chilli, tomato, juice of half the lime and chopped coriander in a bowl. Season to taste.

6 Heat rice according to packet instructions. Place warmed rice into tostada; top with chicken, coriander sprigs, corn, cabbage and salsa. Serve with remaining lime wedges and sour cream.

tips Refrigerate leftover chipotle in a small screw-top jar for up to 1 month. To make a chicken burrito, warm the tortilla and wrap around the filling ingredients. Chipotle in adobo is a hot, smoky-flavoured Mexican sauce made from chipotles (smoke-dried jalapeno chillies). It is available from Mexican and specialist food shops.

Salmon with shaved CAULIFLOWER SALAD

CAULIFLOWER SALAD

PREP & COOK TIME 15 MINUTES   SERVES 1

2½ tablespoons extra virgin olive oil

220g (7 ounces) skinless boneless salmon fillet

1 small clove garlic, crushed

1 anchovy fillet, chopped very finely

1 tablespoon lemon juice

2 tablespoons finely chopped roasted walnuts

1 tablespoon fresh flat-leaf parsley leaves

½ cup (100g) shaved cauliflower

1 Heat 2 teaspoons of the oil in a small frying pan over medium heat. Season salmon with salt, add to pan; cook for 3 minutes on one side, then turn over and cook for a further 1 minute or until just cooked through.

2 Meanwhile, combine remaining ingredients, except the cauliflower, in a small bowl; season to taste.

3 Serve salmon with cauliflower; drizzle with walnut mixture and sprinkle with extra parsley leaves, if you like.

tips Shave the cauliflower using a V-slicer or mandoline. You can accompany the fish with israeli couscous or quinoa, if you like.

Healthy
CHOICE

THE SOUP CAN BE MADE A DAY AHEAD UP TO THE END OF STEP 1.
REFRIGERATE IN AN AIRTIGHT CONTAINER. YOU MAY NEED TO GIVE THE
SOUP A QUICK WHISK IF THE INGREDIENTS ARE SLIGHTLY SEPARATED.

Gazpacho with FETTA AND PRAWNS

PREP & COOK TIME 20 MINUTES SERVES 1

2 medium tomatoes (300g), chopped coarsely

½ medium red capsicum (bell pepper) (200g), chopped coarsely

½ lebanese cucumber (130g), peeled, chopped coarsely

2 green onions (scallions), chopped coarsely

1 small clove garlic, crushed

40g (1½ ounces) sourdough bread, chopped coarsely

¼ cup (60ml) extra virgin olive oil

1½ tablespoons red wine vinegar

1½ cups (375ml) water

6 medium cooked prawns (270g)

2 slices sourdough bread, extra, crusts removed

1 tablespoon olive oil

10g (½ ounce) butter

40g (1½ ounces) fetta, crumbled

1 Blend tomato, capsicum, cucumber, onion, garlic, sourdough, oil, vinegar and the water in a blender for 3 minutes or until smooth. Season to taste.

2 Shell and devein prawns, leaving tails intact.

3 Tear extra sourdough into rough pieces. Heat oil in a small frying pan over medium-high heat, add butter. When butter starts to foam, add bread; cook, tossing frequently, for 2 minutes or until croutons are golden.

4 Pour soup into a bowl. Top with prawns, croutons and fetta. Grind over some freshly ground black pepper, if you like.

tips To maximise the flavour of the soup it's important to use really ripe tomatoes. If you have it on hand you could also sprinkle the soup with some torn dill sprigs or basil leaves.

EXPRESS

FOR

TWO

Lemon grass prawn
AND RICE NOODLES

PREP & COOK TIME 25 MINUTES SERVES 2

12 uncooked large king prawns (shrimp) (840g)

2 tablespoons mirin

2 tablespoons oyster sauce

⅓ cup (80ml) soy sauce

200g (6½ ounces) dried wide rice noodles

1½ tablespoons peanut or vegetable oil

2 teaspoons finely grated fresh ginger

2 cloves garlic, crushed

½ stalk fresh lemon grass, white part only, chopped finely

1 fresh long red chilli, seeded, chopped finely

220g (7 ounces) broccolini, cut into 4cm (1½-inch) lengths

2 green onions (scallions), cut into 4cm (1½-inch) lengths

1 Shell and devein prawns, leaving tails intact.

2 Stir mirin and sauces together in a small bowl.

3 Place noodles in a large heatproof bowl, cover with boiling water; stand until just tender, drain.

4 Heat 2 teaspoons of the oil in a wok over high heat; stir-fry prawns for 2 minutes or until just cooked through. Remove from wok.

5 Add remaining 1 tablespoon of the oil to wok with ginger, garlic, lemon grass, chilli and broccolini; stir-fry for 2 minutes or until broccolini is almost tender.

6 Return prawns to wok with noodles and remaining ingredients; stir-fry until heated through.

tip Serve the noodles topped with thinly sliced green onion and lime wedges if you have them on hand.

IF YOU'D PREFER TO COOK YOUR OWN RICE, DO IT SEVERAL HOURS AHEAD OR THE DAY BEFORE. YOU WILL NEED TO COOK 1 CUP OF RICE, FOLLOWING THE PACKET DIRECTIONS, TO YIELD 3 CUPS OF COOKED RICE, THE EQUIVALENT QUANTITY OF THE PACKAGED RICE IN THE RECIPE. SPREAD THE COOKED RICE IN A SINGLE LAYER OVER A TRAY, COVER AND REFRIGERATE UNTIL NEEDED. REPLACE THE CAPSICUM, CABBAGE AND MUSHROOMS WITH OTHER VEGETABLES YOU HAVE ON HAND; SIMPLY ENSURE THAT THEY ARE CUT INTO THIN SLICES. YOU CAN SPRINKLE THE RICE WITH ASIAN FRIED SHALLOTS FOR ADDED TEXTURE, IF YOU LIKE.

Chicken FRIED RICE

PREP & COOK TIME 25 MINUTES   SERVES 2

2 tablespoons peanut or vegetable oil

2 eggs, beaten lightly

4 chicken thigh fillets (800g), sliced thinly

½ medium red capsicum (bell pepper) (100g), sliced thinly

1 small red onion (100g), sliced thinly

2 cups (160g) coarsely chopped cabbage

150g (5 ounces) oyster mushrooms, chopped coarsely

3 cloves garlic, crushed

½ teaspoon dried chilli flakes

2 x 250g (8-ounces) packaged 90-second microwave white basmati rice

1 teaspoon sesame oil

2 tablespoons soy sauce

2 green onions (scallions), sliced thinly

¼ cup (60ml) sweet chilli sauce

2 tablespoons fresh coriander leaves (cilantro)

1 Heat 1 teaspoon of the oil in a large wok over high heat. Pour egg into wok; cook, tilting wok, until omelette is just set. Remove omelette from wok; chop coarsely.

2 Heat 3 teaspoons of the remaining oil in wok; stir-fry chicken for 2 minutes or until browned. Remove from wok.

3 Heat remaining oil in wok; stir-fry capsicum, half the onion, cabbage, mushrooms, garlic and chilli for 3 minutes or until vegetables soften.

4 Return chicken and egg to wok with rice, sesame oil, soy sauce, onion and 2 tablespoons of the sweet chilli sauce; stir-fry until heated through. (Taste and add extra soy sauce if desired.)

5 Serve rice, drizzled with remaining sweet chilli sauce and sprinkled with coriander and remaining onion.

Lamb koftas WITH SALAD

Healthy CHOICE

POMEGRANATE MOLASSES IS MADE BY COOKING POMEGRANATE JUICE UNTIL IT IS REDUCED AND SYRUPY; IT HAS A SWEET AND SOUR TASTE. IT IS AVAILABLE FROM DELIS AND MIDDLE-EASTERN FOOD STORES. SUBSTITUTE BALSAMIC GLAZE OR HALF AS MUCH RED WINE VINEGAR, IF YOU CAN'T FIND IT.

Lamb koftas
WITH SALAD

PREP & COOK TIME 20 MINUTES SERVES 2

½ teaspoon ground cinnamon

¾ teaspoon ground cumin

1 small brown onion (80g), chopped coarsely

¼ cup fresh flat-leaf parsley leaves

¼ cup fresh mint leaves

300g (9 ounces) minced (ground) lamb

¼ cup fresh flat-leaf parsley leaves, extra

2 cups (140g) coarsely chopped butter (boston) lettuce

4 small red radishes (40g), sliced thinly

2 x 26cm (10.5-inch) round lebanese breads

1 tablespoon pomegranate molasses

⅓ cup (95g) greek-style yoghurt

1 Place spices, onion and herbs in a food processor, season; pulse for 10 seconds or until coarsely chopped. Add lamb, pulse until well combined.

2 Divide mixture into four portions; using wet hands, shape each portion into 12cm (4¾-inch) long koftas (ovals). Thread each kofta onto a metal skewer. Cook koftas in a heated, oiled grill pan or frying pan, turning three times, for 8 minutes or until cooked through.

3 Meanwhile, combine extra parsley with lettuce and radish in a small bowl; divide salad between breads. Serve with koftas, pomegranate molasses and yoghurt.

do-ahead Uncooked koftas can be prepared several hours ahead; refrigerate covered. Uncooked koftas can be frozen for up to 1 month.

tip Metal skewers conduct heat speeding up the cooking time, however you can also use bamboo skewers. It is not necessary to soak them if you are not cooking directly over an open flame.

Sandwich press TOASTIES

Chicken, fig and BLUE CHEESE TOASTIES

PREP & COOK TIME 15 MINUTES **SERVES** 2

Lightly butter 4 slices of wholemeal bread. Place two of the slices, buttered-side down, on a board; divide 2 tablespoons smoky barbecue sauce, 1 cup shredded roast chicken, ¼ sliced small red onion, 2 coarsely chopped dried figs and 60g (2oz) sliced creamy blue castello cheese between slices. Sandwich with remaining bread, buttered-side up. Toast in a sandwich press for 4 minutes or until golden and heated through. Serve with spinach leaves dressed with olive oil and lemon juice.

Bolognese and PARMESAN TOASTIES

PREP & COOK TIME 10 MINUTES **SERVES** 2

Lightly butter 4 slices of sourdough bread. Place two slices, buttered-side down, on a board; divide ⅔ cup store-bought bolognaise sauce, 50g (1½ ounces) sliced parmesan and 2 teaspoons finely chopped fresh oregano between slices. Season. Sandwich with remaining bread, buttered-side up. Toast in a sandwich press for 4 minutes or until golden and heated through. Serve with rocket (arugula) dressed with olive oil and balsamic vinegar.

Smoked salmon
AND EGG TOASTIES

PREP & COOK TIME 15 MINUTES **SERVES** 2

Combine ½ cup spreadable cream cheese, 1 tablespoon chopped fresh dill and 1 teaspoon finely grated lemon rind in a small bowl. Lightly butter 4 slices of white bread. Place two slices, buttered-side down, on a board, spread equally with cream cheese mixture; divide 50g sliced smoked salmon between slices. Cook 2 eggs on a heated, oiled sandwich press for 2 minutes. Place on top of the salmon; sandwich with remaining bread, buttered-side up. Toast in sandwich press for 4 minutes or until golden and heated through. Serve with lemon wedges.

The reuben
TOASTIE

PREP & COOK TIME 15 MINUTES **SERVES** 2

Lightly butter 4 slices of light rye bread. Place two slices, buttered-side down, on a board; divide 2 tablespoons thousand island dressing, 8 slices corned beef, 50g (1½ ounces) sliced dill pickles, ½ cup sauerkraut and 120g (4 ounces) sliced gruyere or cheddar between slices. Season. Sandwich with remaining bread, buttered-side up. Toast in a sandwich press for 4 minutes or until golden and heated through. Serve with dijon mustard.

Healthy CHOICE

IF YOU DON'T HAVE FENNEL SEEDS ON HAND, USE THE SAME QUANTITY OF CORIANDER SEEDS, CRUSHING THEM FIRST WITH A PESTLE AND MORTAR OR THE BASE OF A CLEAN SAUCEPAN. SICILIAN GREEN OLIVES HAVE A MILD BUTTERY TASTE. THEY ARE SOLD IN JARS OR AT THE DELI SECTION OF SUPERMARKETS. IF ONLY UNPITTED OLIVES ARE AVAILABLE, SLICE THE FLESH AWAY FROM THE PITS. USE A MANDOLINE OR V-SLICER TO THINLY SLICE THE FENNEL.

Lamb, fennel & ORANGE SALAD

PREP & COOK TIME 15 MINUTES (& STANDING) **SERVES** 2

1 teaspoon cumin seeds

½ teaspoon fennel seeds

½ teaspoon sea salt flakes

¼ teaspoon freshly ground black pepper

1½ tablespoons extra virgin olive oil

2 lamb backstraps (400g)

1 baby fennel bulb (130g), sliced thinly

75g (1¾ ounces) baby rocket leaves (arugula)

½ cup (60g) pitted sicilian green olives

1 medium orange (240g), halved, sliced thinly

2 teaspoons white wine vinegar

¼ cup (20g) shaved parmesan

1 Combine seeds, salt, pepper and 2 teaspoons of the oil in a medium bowl. Add lamb; turn to coat in mixture.
2 Preheat a grill pan or frying pan over medium-high heat. Add lamb; cook for 2 minutes each side for medium, or until cooked as desired. Remove pan from heat, cover lamb loosely with foil; rest for 5 minutes.
3 Meanwhile, combine remaining ingredients in a medium bowl; season to taste. Cut lamb into slices; serve with salad.

THIS IS AN IDEAL RECIPE TO USE UP LEFTOVER ROAST MEAT.

SUBSTITUTE LAMB, BEEF OR CHICKEN, IF PREFERRED.

Apple & celery
PORCHETTA ROLLS

PREP & COOK TIME 20 MINUTES SERVES 2

⅓ cup (95g) dijonnaise

¼ cup finely chopped fresh flat-leaf parsley

1 small shallot, chopped finely

2 tablespoons olive oil

8 fresh sage leaves

200g (6½ ounces) thickly sliced roast pork

2 italian-style bread rolls (160g)

½ cup baby rocket leaves (arugula)

1 small green apple (130g), cut into matchsticks

2 inner stalks from a bunch of celery with leaves attached, sliced thinly

1 Combine dijonnaise, parsley and shallot in a small bowl.

2 Heat oil in a small frying pan over medium heat. Add sage leaves, cook for 1 minute or until crisp; drain on paper towel. Add pork to the same pan; cook for 2 minutes each side or until pork is lightly browned and heated through. Remove from pan.

3 Add rolls, cut-side down, to same pan; cook for 1½ minutes each side or until toasted.

4 Spread half the dijonnaise mixture over roll bases, top with rocket, warm pork and sage leaves, then combined apple and celery. Spoon over the remaining dijonnaise mixture; sandwich with bread roll lids.

Cheap EAT

Cheddar toasts
WITH VEGETABLE SOUP

PREP & COOK TIME 30 MINUTES SERVES 2

2 teaspoons extra virgin olive oil

1 clove garlic, chopped coarsely

1 small leek (200g), white part only, chopped coarsely

1 trimmed celery stalk (100g), chopped coarsely

2 medium potatoes (400g), diced into 1cm (½-inch) pieces

1 tablespoon fresh lemon thyme leaves

3 cups (750ml) chicken or vegetable stock

⅓ cup (80ml) pouring cream

2 slices prosciutto (30g)

4 slices sourdough bread (200g)

½ cup (60g) grated vintage cheddar

freshly ground black pepper, to serve

1 Preheat oven to 200°C/400°F. Line an oven tray with baking paper.
2 Heat oil in a medium saucepan over medium heat. Add garlic, leek, celery, potato and thyme; cook, stirring, for 2 minutes or until leek softens.
3 Add stock and cream to pan, bring to the boil, reduce heat; simmer, covered for 15 minutes. Season to taste.
4 Meanwhile, place prosciutto and bread slices on tray. Top bread with cheddar. Cook in oven for 8 minutes or until cheddar has melted and prosciutto is crisp.
5 Blend or process soup until smooth. Season with freshly ground black pepper. Serve soup with cheddar toast.

do-ahead Soup can be made a day ahead; reheat just before serving, then toast prosciutto and cheddar toast.

YOU WILL NEED 1 LIME FOR THIS RECIPE. TO ASSIST WITH JUICING, ROLL THE LIME FIRMLY ON A HARD BENCH FIRST. YOU CAN SUBSTITUTE GROUND ALLSPICE WITH ½ TEASPOON GROUND CINNAMON, ¼ TEASPOON GROUND CLOVE AND ¼ TEASPOON GROUND NUTMEG.

Jerk salmon with YOGHURT POTATOES

PREP & COOK TIME 20 MINUTES SERVES 2

Jerk is both the name of the Jamaican dry or wet spice rub used to season fish and chicken; it is also the name of the cooking method. Chilli and allspice are the two defining spices in the rub.

8 baby new potatoes (320g), sliced thickly

⅓ cup firmly packed fresh flat-leaf parsley

⅓ cup firmly packed fresh coriander (cilantro)

1 teaspoon freshly ground black pepper

1 teaspoon dried chilli flakes

1 teaspoon ground allspice

2 cloves garlic, crushed

2 teaspoons finely grated fresh ginger

¼ cup (60ml) lime juice

¼ cup (60ml) extra virgin olive oil

2 x 200g (6½-ounce) skinless, boneless salmon fillets

¼ cup (70g) greek-style yoghurt

2 shallots (50g), chopped finely

1 Boil, steam or microwave potato until tender; cover to keep warm.

2 Reserve 1 tablespoon each of the parsley and coriander. Process remaining herbs with pepper, chilli, allspice, garlic, ginger, juice and oil; season with salt.

3 Pour half the herb mixture over salmon in a medium bowl; stand for 5 minutes.

4 Cook undrained salmon, in a heated medium frying pan, for 2 minutes each side or until just cooked through.

5 Combine potato with yoghurt, shallot and remaining herb mixture. Serve topped with salmon, and sprinkled with reserved herbs.

Healthy CHOICE

USE READY-CHOPPED PUMPKIN FROM SUPERMARKETS AND SOME GREENGROCERS TO SAVE TIME. YOU COULD ALSO MICROWAVE THE PUMPKIN. THE MIXTURE IS QUITE SOFT SO, IF TIME PERMITS, PLACE THE PATTIES INTO THE FREEZER FOR 10 MINUTES TO FIRM BEFORE COOKING.

Pumpkin samosa FRITTERS

PREP & COOK TIME 30 MINUTES SERVES 2

200g (6½ ounces) butternut pumpkin, chopped coarsely

½ x 250g (8-ounce) packet 90-second microwave brown rice, uncooked

¼ cup (30g) frozen peas

1 small carrot (70g), grated coarsely

2 teaspoons curry powder

1 teaspoon finely grated fresh ginger

⅓ cup (25g) dried breadcrumbs

2 tablespoons vegetable oil

⅓ cup (95g) greek-style yoghurt

2 tablespoons hot lime pickle

2 tablespoons fresh mint leaves

1 Cook pumpkin in a medium saucepan of boiling water until tender. Drain, return to the pan; mash until smooth. Stir rice, peas, carrot, curry powder, ginger and breadcrumbs into pumpkin. Season.

2 Using oiled hands, form 6 x ¼ cups of mixture into patties. Heat oil in a large frying pan over medium heat. Cook patties, in batches, for 2 minutes each side or until golden. Serve with yoghurt, pickle and mint leaves. Accompany with a spinach and tomato salad, if you like.

tip An Indian speciality, lime pickle is a mixed pickle condiment of limes that adds a hot and spicy taste to meals; it is available in Indian food shops.

Pineapple huli huli CHICKEN WINGS

Pineapple *huli huli* CHICKEN WINGS

PREP & COOK TIME 35 MINUTES SERVES 2

This tangy Hawaiian chicken recipe is traditionally cooked in a double grill, suspended over a charcoal barbecue. Huli means 'turn' in Hawaiian, a reference to motorised or manual turning of the grill during cooking.

⅓ cup (80ml) fresh pineapple juice

¼ cup (60ml) tomato sauce (ketchup)

¼ cup (60ml) soy sauce

2 tablespoons malt vinegar

2 teaspoons finely grated fresh ginger

1 clove garlic, crushed

2 tablespoons brown sugar

2 teaspoons paprika

8 chicken wings (800g) (see tips)

pineapple and chilli salad

400g (12½ ounces) pineapple, core removed, chopped coarsely

1 lebanese cucumber (130g), chopped coarsely

1 fresh long green chilli, sliced thinly

½ small red onion (50g), sliced thinly (or 1 spring onion, thinly sliced)

2 tablespoons lime juice

½ cup each fresh coriander (cilantro) and mint leaves

1 Preheat oven to 220°C/425°F. Line a large oven tray with baking paper.
2 Place pineapple juice, sauces, vinegar, ginger, garlic and sugar in a medium frying pan; boil, over medium heat, for 5 minutes or until sauce is slightly thickened.
3 Place chicken on oven tray, sprinkle with paprika; toss to combine. Add sauce; toss to combine. Transfer tray to oven; roast chicken, basting occasionally, for 25 minutes or until golden and cooked through.
4 Meanwhile, make pineapple and chilli salad.
5 Serve huli huli chicken with pineapple and chilli salad; accompany with extra lime wedges, if you like.

pineapple and chilli salad Combine ingredients in a large bowl; toss gently to combine.

tips You can cook the chicken wings whole, if preferred. To prepare wings, snip the tips off using strong kitchen scissors, then cut the wings in half at the joint with the scissors or a large flat knife. You could also ask the butcher to do this for you. Any leftovers will make a great lunch the next day.

RAVIOLI IS AVAILABLE FROM THE REFRIGERATED SECTION OF MOST SUPERMARKETS. FOR A VEGETARIAN MINESTRONE, USE SPINACH AND RICOTTA RAVIOLI. IF FREEZING THE SOUP, DON'T ADD THE RAVIOLI. SPRINKLE THE SOUP WITH A PINCH OF DRIED CHILLI FLAKES IF YOU DON'T HAVE CHILLI OIL.

Minestrone with
BEEF RAVIOLI

PREP & COOK TIME 25 MINUTES   SERVES 2

2 teaspoons extra virgin olive oil

½ small brown onion (40g), chopped finely

1 clove garlic, crushed

2 teaspoons finely chopped fresh rosemary leaves

1 small carrot (70g), chopped finely

1 trimmed celery stalk (100g), chopped finely

400g (12½ ounces) canned diced tomatoes

2 cups (500ml) vegetable stock

1 teaspoon caster (superfine) sugar

150g (4½ ounces) fresh beef ravioli

2 tablespoons shaved parmesan

1 teaspoon chilli oil (see tips)

1 tablespoon fresh flat-leaf parsley leaves

crusty bread, to serve

1 Heat oil in a medium saucepan over medium heat. Cook onion, garlic, rosemary, carrot and celery for 5 minutes or until softened.

2 Add tomatoes, stock and sugar; season. Bring to the boil; cook for 5 minutes. Add ravioli, cook for 5 minutes or until ravioli is tender.

3 Divide soup and ravioli among bowls. Top with parmesan, chilli oil and parsley; accompany with bread.

FOR A VEGETARIAN OPTION, SPRINKLE HALOUMI SLICES WITH ZA'ATAR AND PAN-FRY OVER MEDIUM HEAT FOR 1 MINUTE EACH SIDE. ZA'ATAR IS A MIDDLE EASTERN SPICE BLEND OFTEN CONTAINING THYME, SUMAC, SESAME SEEDS AND SALT. IT IS AVAILABLE FROM MAJOR SUPERMARKETS AND DELIS. TO MAKE YOUR OWN, COMBINE 1 TEASPOON DRIED THYME WITH ½ TEASPOON LIGHTLY CRUSHED SESAME SEEDS AND ¼ TEASPOON EACH SUMAC AND SALT.

Za'atar chicken SCHNITZEL AND SALAD

PREP & COOK TIME 30 MINUTES SERVES 2

2 x 200g (6½ ounce) fresh crumbed chicken schnitzels

2 teaspoons za'atar (see tips)

2 tablespoons red wine vinegar

1 tablespoon extra virgin olive oil

2 teaspoons honey

1 clove garlic, crushed

6 trimmed red radishes (90g), sliced thinly

125g (4 ounces) cherry tomatoes, halved

1 lebanese cucumber (130g), chopped coarsely

400g (12½ ounces) canned chickpeas (garbanzos), rinsed, drained

½ cup fresh mint leaves

2 lemon wedges

2 pitta breads

1 Preheat oven to 200°C/400°F. Line an oven tray with baking paper.

2 Place schnitzel on tray, sprinkle with za'atar. Bake for 12 minutes or until golden. Stand for 5 minutes then slice thickly.

3 Meanwhile, combine vinegar, oil, honey and garlic in a large bowl; season. Add radish, tomato, cucumber, chickpeas and mint; toss gently to combine.

4 Serve salad with schnitzel, lemon wedges and pitta bread.

Pineapple
PORK STIR-FRY

PORK STIR-FRY

PREP & COOK TIME 25 MINUTES   SERVES 2

250g (8 ounce) canned pineapple pieces in natural juice

200g (6½ ounces) pork fillet, sliced thinly

2 teaspoons finely grated fresh ginger

1 tablespoon light soy sauce

2 teaspoons sriracha chilli sauce

1 clove garlic, crushed

2 tablespoons vegetable oil

220g (7 ounces) shelf fresh udon noodles

210g (6½ ounces) broccolini, sliced

1 small brown onion (80g), sliced thinly

1 fresh long red chilli, sliced thinly

125g (4 ounces) baby corn, halved lengthways

¼ cup (60ml) water

2 tablespoons chopped salted roasted peanuts

1 Drain pineapple juice into a medium bowl; reserve the pineapple. Add pork, ginger, sauces, garlic and 1 tablespoon of the oil to the bowl; stir to combine. Stand for 10 minutes.

2 Place noodles in a heatproof bowl, cover with boiling water. Stir using tongs to separate noodles, stand for 1 minute; drain.

3 Drain pork from marinade, reserve marinade. Heat 2 teaspoons of the oil in a wok or large frying pan over medium-high heat; stir-fry pork for 2 minutes or until browned. Remove from pan.

4 Heat remaining oil in wok, add broccolini, onion, chilli and corn; stir-fry for 3 minutes or until tender. Add reserved marinade and water; bring to the boil. Add pineapple, noodles and pork; stir-fry for 1 minute. Divide into bowls; sprinkle with peanuts to serve.

tips You could also use hokkien noodles. Sriracha is a thai-style chilli sauce available from selected supermarkets and Asian food stores. Substitute with whatever chilli sauce you have on hand, or use a little fresh seeded chilli.

IF YOU DON'T HAVE A LARGE GRILL PLATE, YOU CAN COOK THE QUESADILLAS IN A LARGE SANDWICH PRESS FOR 8 MINUTES, OR IN A PREHEATED 200°C/400°F OVEN FOR 15 MINUTES.

Pickled chillies with CHICKEN QUESADILLA

PREP & COOK TIME 30 MINUTES **SERVES** 2

1 large chicken breast (260g), halved horizontally

2 tablespoons olive oil

1 teaspoon finely grated lime rind

2 tablespoons lime juice

2 cloves garlic, grated finely

1 cob corn (400g)

4 x 15cm (6-inch) flour tortillas (100g)

½ cup (120g) sour cream

½ cup (60g) coarsely grated cheddar

2 tablespoons fresh coriander (cilantro) sprigs

2 tablespoons sour cream, extra

quick pickled chillies

¼ cup (60ml) apple cider vinegar

1 tablespoon caster (superfine) sugar

2 fresh long green chillies, sliced thinly

1 Make quick pickled chillies.

2 Heat a large grill pan (or barbecue) over medium heat.

3 Combine chicken in a small bowl with oil, rind, juice and garlic; season. Cook chicken for 2 minutes each side or until cooked through; cool slightly, then shred coarsely. Grill corn, turning occasionally, for 8 minutes or until charred; cool slightly, then remove kernels from cob using a small sharp knife.

4 Spread tortillas with sour cream, top two tortillas with cheddar, corn and chicken, season; top with remaining tortillas, pressing down gently.

5 Cook quesadilla for 4 minutes each side or until tortillas are lightly charred and filling is warmed through. Serve with pickled chilli, coriander and extra sour cream.

quick pickled chillies Combine vinegar and sugar in a small bowl; stir to combine. Add chillies; stand for 10 minutes to pickle.

Bacon, cider
AND FENNEL MUSSELS

PREP & COOK TIME 15 MINUTES SERVES 2

Serve these mussels steamed in cider with plenty of crusty bread to mop up the cooking juices, or Belgian style, with thin chips and mayonnaise.

1 tablespoon olive oil

1 rindless bacon slice (80g), chopped coarsely

2 cloves garlic, sliced thinly

1 baby fennel bulb (130g), sliced thinly, fronds reserved

1kg (2 pounds) pot-ready mussels (see tips)

¾ cup (180ml) dry cider

crusty bread, to serve

1 Heat oil in a large saucepan over medium heat. Cook bacon, garlic and fennel, stirring frequently, for 3 minutes or until browned. Add mussels and cider, bring to the boil. Cover pan with a lid, cook, shaking the pan occasionally, for 5 minutes or until mussels start to open. Top with reserved fennel fronds, and serve with bread.

tips Pot-ready, or pre-bagged, mussels are generally sold cleaned and ready to use. If you have bought loose mussels, scrub the shells to remove the debris, then remove the beard, the hair-like byssal thread, by yanking it down.
It was once thought that mussels that didn't open were bad so recipes instructed the cook to discard them; we now know this is simply not true. If a mussel refuses to open, it is simply due to the adductor muscle, which usually hold the two halves of the shell shut, reacting to the heat. If you want to, prise the shells open with a blunt knife.

IF COOKING THE SKEWERS IN A GRILL PAN IT IS NOT NECESSARY TO SOAK THEM FIRST. HOWEVER, IF YOU ARE BARBECUING ON A GRILL WITH A LIVE FLAME, YOU WILL NEED TO SOAK THEM TO STOP THEM FROM SCORCHING OR BURNING WHILE COOKING. PLACE SKEWERS IN A TALL JUG, FILL WITH BOILING WATER FROM THE KETTLE AND SOAK FOR 5 MINUTES; DRAIN.

Greek pork skewers with CRUSHED WHITE BEANS

PREP & COOK TIME 30 MINUTES SERVES 2

2 tablespoons extra virgin olive oil

1 medium onion (150g), sliced thinly

1 clove garlic, sliced thinly

½ cup (125ml) dry white wine

600g (1¼ pound) canned white beans, rinsed, drained

1 cup (250ml) chicken stock

2 tablespoons lemon juice

2 tablespoons coarsely chopped fresh oregano

1 teaspoon finely grated lemon rind

2 cloves garlic, halved, extra

2 tablespoons red wine vinegar

2½ tablespoons loosely packed fresh oregano leaves, extra

350g (11 ounces) pork fillet, diced into 3cm (1¼-inch) pieces

2 tablespoons fresh flat-leaf parsley

lemon wedges, to serve

1 Heat 1 tablespoon of the oil in a saucepan over medium heat. Add onion and sliced garlic to pan; cook, stirring, for 6 minutes or until tender. Add wine, stir to combine; add beans and stock. Bring to a simmer; cook, stirring occasionally, for 15 minutes or until thickened. Crush beans with a fork, stir in lemon juice and chopped oregano; season to taste. Cover to keep warm.

2 Meanwhile, process remaining oil, rind, halved garlic, vinegar and extra oregano until mixture forms a paste; season. Combine pork and oregano mixture in a medium bowl; thread pork onto skewers.

3 Heat an oiled grill pan (or grill or barbecue) over medium heat; cook skewers, turning occasionally, for 6 minutes or until cooked through. Serve with crushed beans, sprinkle with parsley, accompany with wedges.

Grilled mozzarella
AND SALAMI PIADINA

PREP & COOK TIME 25 MINUTES   SERVES 2

Piadina is a super quick-to-make un-yeasted flatbread, originating in Romagna in northern Italy. Once you've mastered this version, adjust the toppings to what you have on hand. The salami we used was only mildly spiced, making this recipe 'kid friendly'.

200g (1⅓ cups) plain (all-purpose) flour

½ teaspoon bicarbonate of soda (baking soda)

1 teaspoon salt

⅓ cup (80ml) water

⅓ cup (80ml) olive oil

1 clove garlic, halved

200g (6½ ounces) cherry tomatoes, halved

½ cup fresh basil leaves, torn coarsely

1 tablespoon red wine vinegar

1 ball buffalo mozzarella (120g), torn

12 thin slices spicy salami

1 Combine flour, soda and salt in a bowl, add water and ¼ cup oil; stir to form a dough. Transfer to a floured work surface; knead for 2 minutes or until smooth. Divide into two balls; roll each ball into a 3mm-thick (⅛-inch), 24cm x 16cm (9½-inch x 6½-inch) oval.

2 Heat an oiled grill pan (or a frying pan) over high heat. Cook piadina for 2 minutes each side or until lightly charred and cooked through. Rub with garlic and season with salt.

3 Combine tomato, basil, vinegar and remaining oil in a medium bowl; season to taste. Top piadina with tomato mixture, salami and mozzarella; season to taste. Drizzle with a little extra oil before serving, if you like.

serving suggestion Rocket salad.

tip Basil is a herb that dislikes the cold, so it tends to blacken and shrivel if stored in the fridge. Instead, treat it like a bunch of flowers: snip the ends slightly and place the bunch of basil in a jug with the water reaching halfway up the stems.

KID FRIENDLY

Healthy
CHOICE

Prawns with
RISONI AND PEAS

PREP & COOK TIME 20 MINUTES **SERVES** 2

20g (¾ ounce) butter, chopped

2 cloves garlic, crushed

½ cup (125ml) chicken stock

½ cup (125ml) water

2½ cups (300g) frozen peas

1 cup (220g) risoni pasta

2 tablespoons extra virgin olive oil

12 medium shelled uncooked prawns (540g), tails intact

¼ cup coarsely chopped fresh flat-leaf parsley

1 fresh long red chilli, seeded, chopped finely

2 teaspoons extra virgin olive oil, extra

lemon wedges, to serve

1 Heat butter in a small saucepan over low heat. Once foaming, add half the garlic; cook, stirring, until lightly golden. Add stock and the water, bring to the boil; reduce heat slightly. Add peas; cook, covered, for 3 minutes or until tender. Remove and reserve ½ cup peas.

2 Cook risoni in a saucepan of boiling water until almost tender; drain.

3 Meanwhile, heat oil in a large frying pan over high heat. Cook prawns for 1 minute, add remaining garlic, turn prawns over; cook for a further minute or until just cooked through.

4 Using a stick blender (or small food processor), coarsely puree pea and stock mixture; stir in reserved whole peas. Season to taste. Add puree mixture and risoni to pan with prawns; stir to combine. Cook for a further minute or until heated through. Stir in parsley and chilli.

5 To serve, divide mixture between bowls, drizzle with extra oil; accompany with wedges.

tips The recipe can easily be doubled to serve four. You could make the recipe using vongole (clams) instead of prawns and moghrabieh (pearl couscous) instead of the risoni. Accompany with crusty bread.

Angel hair pasta with
FRESH TOMATO SAUCE

BUFFALO MOZZARELLA HAS A MORE TANGY, LACTIC DAIRY TASTE THAN
COW'S MILK MOZZARELLA, WHICH CAN BE USED INSTEAD.

Angel hair pasta with
FRESH TOMATO SAUCE

PREP & COOK TIME 25 MINUTES SERVES 2

¼ cup (60ml) extra virgin olive oil

2 cloves garlic, chopped finely

6 medium firm tomatoes (900g), halved, grated coarsely

1½ teaspoons caster (superfine) sugar

1 cup fresh basil leaves, torn

250g (8 ounces) angel hair pasta

120g (4 ounces) green beans

1 small jar (150g) marinated artichoke hearts, quartered

125g (4 ounces) buffalo mozzarella

2 teaspoons extra virgin olive oil, extra

1 Heat oil in a large saucepan over medium heat. Add garlic, tomato, sugar and half the basil; stir well to combine. Cook for 10 minutes to allow flavours to infuse. Season to taste.

2 Meanwhile, cook pasta and beans in a large saucepan of boiling water until pasta is almost cooked; drain, cut beans in half crossways.

3 Add artichokes and pasta to pan with sauce; toss gently to combine.

4 Divide pasta between bowls, tear mozzarella over top; sprinkle with remaining basil, and drizzle with extra oil.

One PAN

Spiced seafood
COCONUT CURRY

200g (6½ ounces) vongole (clams)

1 small bunch fresh coriander (cilantro)

1 tablespoon vegetable oil

½ teaspoon ground cumin

1 teaspoon ground turmeric

1 baby fennel bulb (130g), sliced thinly

270ml can coconut milk

¾ cup (180ml) chicken stock or water

3 teaspoons fish sauce

2 teaspoons caster (superfine) sugar

2 teaspoons lime juice, plus extra wedges to serve

6 large, shelled uncooked prawns, tails intact

250g (8 ounces) firm white fish fillets, cut into 3cm (1¼-inch) pieces

1 lime, cut into wedges

1 Soak vongole in a medium bowl of cold water for 3 minutes; drain. Trim roots from coriander leaving 2cm (¾-inch) stem attached, wash well then chop finely. Pick ¼ cup coriander leaves. (Reserve remaining coriander for another recipe.)

2 Heat oil in a large saucepan over medium heat. Cook spices, fennel and coriander root, stirring, for 4 minutes or until fragrant and lightly caramelised.

3 Increase heat to high; add vongole to pan, stir to combine then cover with a lid. Cook for 2 minutes, shaking the pan occasionally, or until vongole open. Remove vongole and set aside.

4 Stir coconut milk and stock into pan; bring to the boil. Stir in fish sauce, sugar and lime juice. Add remaining seafood; cook, stirring, for 2 minutes or until just cooked through. Return vongole to pan.

5 Divide curry between bowls, sprinkle with coriander sprigs, and accompany with lime wedges.

serving suggestion Steamed basmati rice or flatbread, such as naan or paratha.

tip Use firm white fish fillets that will hold together during cooking, such as snapper or blue eye trevalla.

SO YOU DON'T HAVE TO SEPARATE THE GREEN BEANS FROM THE KUMARA AFTER COOKING, PLACE A
METAL SIEVE INTO THE SAUCEPAN AND ADD THE GREEN BEANS TO THAT, THEN COOK AS INSTRUCTED.

Veal cutlets with
KUMARA MASH & BEANS

PREP & COOK TIME 30 MINUTES   SERVES 2

1 large kumara (orange sweet potato) (500g), cut into
3cm (1¼-inch) pieces

200g (6½ ounces) green beans, trimmed

40g (1½ ounces) butter, chopped

2 tablespoons olive oil

2 frenched veal cutlets (250g)

1 clove garlic, thinly sliced

125g (4 ounces) cherry tomatoes, quartered

2 tablespoons pesto

1 Place kumara in a medium saucepan of cold water and
bring to the boil, reduce heat; cook, covered, for 8 minutes.
Add green beans; cook a further 2 minutes or until tender.
Drain; separate beans from kumara. Return kumara to pan;
mash with butter until smooth. Season to taste; cover to
keep warm. Halve beans lengthways.

2 Meanwhile, heat half the oil in a medium frying pan over
medium-high heat. Cook veal for 5 minutes each side for
medium or until cooked to your liking. Remove from pan;
rest, loosely covered with foil, for 5 minutes.

3 Heat remaining oil in same pan over medium heat. Add
garlic and beans; cook for 1 minute or until garlic is lightly
golden. Season to taste.

4 Serve veal with mash, bean mixture, tomato and pesto.

Salt & pepper tofu
WITH SOBA NOODLES

PREP & COOK TIME 20 MINUTES   SERVES 2

300g (9½ ounce) block medium tofu

1 tablespoon sesame oil

1 tablespoon rice flour

1 tablespoon sesame seeds

1 teaspoon ground white pepper

½ teaspoon freshly ground black pepper

½ teaspoon sea salt

180g (5½ ounces) soba noodles

170g (5½ ounces) asparagus trimmed, halved crosswise on the diagonal

vegetable oil, for shallow-frying

⅓ cup (80ml) teriyaki sauce

1 medium lebanese cucumber (170g), halved lengthwise and crosswise, seeds removed, thinly sliced

1 green onion (scallion), sliced thinly

½ teaspoon sesame oil, extra

1 Line a plate with paper towel. Place tofu on top, place another piece of paper towel and a plate on top of tofu. Stand for 10 minutes to drain.

2 Meanwhile, place sesame oil on a small plate. Combine flour, sesame seeds, pepper and salt in a small shallow bowl.

3 Bring a medium saucepan of water to the boil; cook noodles for 1 minute. Add asparagus to noodles; cook for a further 3 minutes or until tender. Drain.

4 Cut tofu into 6 cubes; lightly coat each cube in sesame oil, then coat in rice flour mixture.

5 Heat 1.5cm (¾-inch) oil in a small frying pan over medium heat. Shallow-fry tofu, in two batches, for 2 minutes each side until golden.

6 Meanwhile, warm teriyaki sauce in same medium pan over medium heat. Add noodles, asparagus and cucumber to pan; stir until warmed through.

7 Divide noodle mixture between bowls. Top with tofu and onion; drizzle with extra sesame oil to serve.

Chana dhal with
CHUTNEY YOGHURT

CHUTNEY YOGHURT

PREP & COOK TIME 30 MINUTES SERVES 2

Our dhal recipe deliberately makes double the amount you will eat so you aren't left with half-opened cans. Instead you will be able to take the following night off cooking, or take the leftovers to work for lunch.

1 tablespoon peanut oil

1 large brown onion (200g), sliced thinly

1½ teaspoons finely grated fresh ginger

2 teaspoons brown sugar

⅓ cup (75g) korma curry paste

1 teaspoon each ground cumin, turmeric and sweet paprika

400g (12 ounces) canned diced tomatoes

250g (8 ounces) cherry tomatoes

1 cup (250ml) water

1 cup (250ml) coconut milk

400g (12½ ounces) canned brown lentils, rinsed, drained

400g (12½ ounces) canned chickpeas (garbanzo beans), rinsed, drained

2 tablespoons fresh coriander (cilantro)

chutney yoghurt

⅔ cup (190g) greek-style yoghurt

1 tablespoon mango chutney

1 Heat oil in a large saucepan over medium heat; cook onion, ginger and sugar, stirring, until soft. Add paste and spices; cook, stirring, until fragrant.
2 Add canned tomatoes, cherry tomatoes, the water, coconut milk, lentils and chickpeas to pan; bring to the boil. Reduce heat, simmer, uncovered, for 10 minutes or until mixture has thickened slightly.
3 Meanwhile, make chutney yoghurt.
4 Serve dhal sprinkled with coriander and dollops of chutney yoghurt.
chutney yoghurt Swirl ingredients together in a small bowl.

serving suggestion Warm roti bread.

tip Freeze individual portions of dhal in airtight containers for up to 1 month. Thaw the dhal overnight in the fridge. If taking the dhal to work, reheat thawed dhal in the microwave at work. Chutney yoghurt is not suitable to freeze. Pack chutney in a separate airtight container if taking to work.

EXPRESS

for the

FAMILY

Crumbed chicken
WITH SPICY MAYONNAISE

PREP & COOK TIME 25 MINUTES   SERVES 4

2 teaspoons finely grated lemon rind

¼ cup coarsely chopped fresh flat-leaf parsley

½ cup (40g) finely grated parmesan

1 cup (75g) japanese (panko) breadcrumbs

½ cup (75g) plain (all-purpose) flour

2 eggs

12 chicken tenderloins (900g)

vegetable oil, for shallow-frying

3 cups (75g) mixed salad leaves

2 teaspoons lemon juice

lemon wedges, to serve

spicy mayonnaise

¾ teaspoon piri piri seasoning

2 teaspoons lemon juice

⅔ cup (200g) whole-egg mayonnaise

1 Make spicy mayonnaise.

2 Place lemon rind, parsley, parmesan and breadcrumbs in a shallow bowl. In another shallow bowl, place flour; season. In a third shallow bowl; lightly beat eggs. Dust chicken in flour, then dip in egg, allowing excess to drip off, then coat in breadcrumb mixture.

3 Heat 1cm (½-inch) oil in a large frying pan over medium heat; shallow-fry chicken, in batches, for 1 minute each side or until golden and cooked through. Remove with a slotted spoon; drain on paper towel.

4 Toss salad leaves with lemon juice and serve with chicken; accompany with mayonnaise and lemon wedges.

spicy mayonnaise Combine ingredients in a small bowl; season to taste.

Cheap
EAT

IT IS NOT NECESSARY TO ADD OIL TO THE FRYING PAN WHEN COOKING THE CHORIZO AS SUFFICIENT FAT WILL BE RELEASED FROM THE SAUSAGES DURING COOKING.

Rigatoni with arrabbiata AND CHORIZO SAUCE

PREP & COOK TIME 25 MINUTES SERVES 4

500g (1 pound) penne or rigatoni pasta

3 cured chorizo sausages (300g), sliced thinly

2 tablespoons extra virgin olive oil

1 large onion (200g), chopped finely

1 teaspoon dried chilli flakes

3 cloves garlic, crushed

700ml bottle passata (sieved pureed tomato)

1 cup (250ml) water

½ teaspoon brown sugar

½ cup coarsely chopped fresh flat-leaf parsley

⅔ cup (50g) finely grated parmesan

1 Cook pasta in a large saucepan of boiling water until almost tender; drain, return to pan.

2 Meanwhile, cook chorizo in a large frying pan over medium-high heat, turning occasionally, for 2 minutes or until chorizo is browned; remove from pan, drain on paper towel.

3 Add oil to same frying pan; cook onion, chilli and garlic, stirring, for 3 minutes or until onion has softened. Add passata, the water and sugar. Bring to the boil, reduce heat to low; simmer, stirring occasionally, for 7 minutes or until the sauce has thickened slightly. Season to taste with salt.

4 Add sauce to pasta in pan with parsley; stir over medium heat until heated through. Stir in parmesan.

Thai fish burgers
WITH PICKLED VEGETABLES

Thai fish burgers
WITH PICKLED VEGETABLES

PREP & COOK TIME 30 MINUTES SERVES 4

2 lebanese cucumbers (260g)

1 large carrot (180g)

2 fresh long red chillies, sliced thinly

2 tablespoons caster (superfine) sugar

2 tablespoons white vinegar

600g (1¼ pounds) red fish fillets

2 tablespoons thai red curry paste

2 tablespoons fish sauce

4 fresh kaffir lime leaves, sliced thinly

6 green beans, sliced thinly

1 egg

½ cup fresh coriander leaves (cilantro)

2 tablespoons peanut or vegetable oil

4 large bread rolls, split horizontally

⅓ cup (80ml) sweet chilli sauce

1 Using a mandoline, V-slicer or wide vegetable peeler, thinly slice cucumber and carrot lengthways into long ribbons. Combine cucumber, carrot, chilli, sugar and vinegar in a medium bowl. Stand for 10 minutes or until vegetables have softened, turning every few minutes. Drain.

2 Meanwhile, pulse fish, paste, fish sauce, lime leaves, beans, egg and half the coriander in a food processor for 1 minute or until smooth. Using oiled hands, shape mixture into four 12cm (4¾-inch) patties.

3 Heat oil in a large frying pan over medium heat. Cook patties for 2 minutes each side or until cooked through. Drain on paper towel.

4 Add bread rolls, cut-side down, to same frying pan; cook for 1 minute or until lightly toasted.

5 Sandwich rolls with fish burgers, sweet chilli sauce, pickled vegetables and remaining coriander.

do-ahead Fish patties can be prepared several hours ahead; store, covered, in the fridge until ready to cook.

tip To use kaffir lime leaves, fold a leaf in half and cut out the tough centre vein. Kaffir lime leaves will keep in an airtight container in the fridge for two weeks or can be frozen for up to 1 month. Use straight from the freezer.

Rice cooker mac
FOUR WAYS

Cauliflower
MAC & CHEESE

PREP & COOK TIME 25 MINUTES **SERVES** 4

Cut half a cauliflower into florets; place into the bowl
of a rice cooker with 300g (9½oz) macaroni, 2½ cups
boiling water and 1 teaspoon salt; stir to combine. Set
rice cooker to regular cook. Cook, covered, for 8 minutes
or until water is almost absorbed and pasta is slightly firm.
Stir in 1 cup milk, 300ml thickened cream, 2 teaspoons
dijon mustard, 200g (6½oz) grated vintage cheddar and
100g (3oz) grated mozzarella. Cook for a further 5 minutes;
season. (The sauce will look wet but it will thicken on
standing). Divide into bowls; sprinkle with ⅓ cup toasted
pumpkin seeds (pepitas) and 2 tablespoons coarsely
chopped fresh flat-leaf parsley.

Broccoli mac
& BLUE CHEESE

PREP & COOK TIME 25 MINUTES **SERVES** 4

Cut 400g (12½oz) broccoli into florets; place into
the bowl of a rice cooker with 300g (9½oz) macaroni,
2½ cups boiling water and 1 teaspoon salt, stir to combine.
Set rice cooker to regular cook. Cook, covered, for about
8 minutes or until water is almost absorbed and pasta is
slightly firm. Stir in 1 cup milk, 250g (8oz) crème fraîche,
2 teaspoons dijon mustard, 200g (6½oz) grated vintage
cheddar and 100g (3oz) mild-tasting blue cheese. Cook
for a further 5 minutes; season. (The sauce will look wet
but will thicken on standing). Divide into bowls; sprinkle
with ⅓ cup coarsely chopped dry roasted almonds.

Mexican
MAC ATTACK

PREP & COOK TIME 25 MINUTES **SERVES** 4

Place 300g (9½oz) macaroni, 2½ cups boiling water and 1 teaspoon salt into the bowl of a rice cooker; stir to combine. Set rice cooker to regular cook. Cook, covered, for 8 minutes or until water is almost absorbed and pasta is slightly firm. Meanwhile, drain 225g (7oz) bottled piquillo peppers. Slice peppers coarsely, then stir into macaroni mixture with 1 cup milk, 300g sour cream, 200g (6½oz) grated vintage cheddar, 100g (3oz) mozzarella, ½ teaspoon each ground cumin and smoked paprika. Cook for a further 5 minutes; season. (The sauce will look wet but will thicken on standing). Divide into bowls; sprinkle 1 cup crushed corn chips and ¼ cup fresh coriander leaves.

Greek
MAC & CHEESE

PREP & COOK TIME 25 MINUTES **SERVES** 4

Place 300g (9½oz) macaroni, 2½ cups boiling water and 1 teaspoon salt into the bowl of a rice cooker; stir to combine. Set rice cooker to regular cook. Cook, covered, for 8 minutes or until water is almost absorbed and pasta is slightly firm. Stir in ¾ cup milk, 300ml pouring cream, 200g (6½oz) grated mozzarella and 100g (3oz) crumbled fetta. Cook for a further 5 minutes; season. (The sauce will look wet but will thicken on standing). Stir in 2 cups baby spinach until wilted. Divide into bowls. Combine 2 tablespoons coarsely chopped fresh dill and 1 teaspoon zested lemon rind in a small bowl, then sprinkle over mac and cheese.

Healthy CHOICE

Fennel-crusted pork
FILLETS WITH PEARS

PREP & COOK TIME 30 MINUTES   SERVES 4

350g (11 ounces) broccolini, trimmed

2 tablespoons extra virgin olive oil

20g (¾ ounce) butter

2 small pears (360g), cored, halved

4 pork fillets (960g)

1 teaspoon freshly ground black pepper

2 teaspoons fennel seeds

1 tablespoon wholegrain mustard

½ cup (125ml) chicken stock

½ cup (125ml) pear juice

1 Boil, steam or microwave broccolini until just tender; drain, return to pan with 1 tablespoon of the olive oil. Season to taste, toss to combine; cover to keep warm.

2 Heat butter in a medium frying pan over medium heat; cook pears for 3 minutes or until browned and just tender. Remove from pan; cover to keep warm.

3 Meanwhile, combine pork, pepper, fennel, half the mustard and remaining olive oil in a medium bowl. Cook pork in same pan, turning occasionally, for 5 minutes each side or until just cooked through. Remove pork from pan; cover loosely with foil.

4 Drain excess fat from pan. Return pan to heat; add stock and juice, simmer for 2 minutes or until mixture thickens slightly. Stir in remaining mustard.

5 Serve pork with pears, mustard jus and broccolini.

tip For a recipe variation, use chicken in place of pork and apples in place of pears.

Pasta ribbons
WITH SMOKED TROUT

TO PREVENT THE PASTA STICKING TOGETHER, DON'T BE TEMPTED TO ADD OLIVE OIL TO THE WATER, IT DOESN'T HELP AND WILL BE DRAINED AWAY WITH THE COOKING WATER. INSTEAD, ENSURE THE POT IS VERY LARGE AND THE WATER BOILING RAPIDLY, STIR THE PASTA IMMEDIATELY FOR A FEW SECONDS; DOING THIS SHOULD BE SUFFICIENT TO KEEP RIBBONS SEPARATE. ONCE DRAINED, IF YOU ARE NOT USING IT IMMEDIATELY, YOU CAN TOSS THE PASTA WITH A LITTLE OLIVE OIL TO PREVENT IT STICKING.

Pasta ribbons WITH SMOKED TROUT

PREP & COOK TIME 25 MINUTES SERVES 6

500g (1 pound) curly ribbon pasta

2 x 350g (11 ounces) hot smoked whole trout

⅓ cup (80ml) extra virgin olive oil

2 medium red onions (340g), sliced thinly

3 cloves garlic, crushed

3 large zucchini (450g), cut into long thin strips

1 tablespoon finely grated lemon rind

⅓ cup (80ml) lemon juice

½ cup coarsely chopped fresh dill

¾ cup (60g) shaved parmesan

1 Cook pasta in a large saucepan of boiling water until almost tender; drain.
2 Meanwhile, remove flesh from trout in large chunks, discarding skin and bones.
3 Heat 1 tablespoon of the oil in a large saucepan; cook onion and garlic, stirring, for 2 minutes or until onion starts to soften.
4 Return pasta to saucepan with trout, zucchini, remaining olive oil, rind, juice, dill and half the parmesan; stir over low heat until heated through. Season to taste.
5 Serve pasta topped with remaining parmesan.

tip Use a julienne peeler to cut the zucchini into strips; or cut it into ribbons using a regular vegetable peeler, then cut into thin strips.

Steak & spuds
WITH SALSA VERDE

PREP & COOK TIME 30 MINUTES SERVES 4

1½ tablespoons olive oil

500g (1 pound) small kipfler (fingerling) potatoes, halved lengthways

8 x 100g (3 ounces) beef fillet medallions

1 bunch watercress (350g) trimmed

salsa verde

1 clove garlic, crushed

1 teaspoon dijon mustard

2 teaspoons baby capers

2 anchovy fillets

3 teaspoons red wine vinegar

3 cornichons

¼ cup loosely packed fresh mint leaves

¼ cup loosely packed fresh basil leaves

2 tablespoons coarsely chopped fresh flat-leaf parsley

¼ cup (60ml) extra virgin olive oil

1 Preheat oven to 220°C/425°F.

2 Line an oven tray with baking paper. Toss potatoes with half the oil on the tray; season. Roast potato for 20 minutes or until golden and tender.

3 Make salsa verde.

4 Heat remaining oil over medium-high heat in a large frying pan; cook beef, 2½ minutes each side for medium, or until cooked as desired.

5 Serve steak with potatoes, watercress and salsa verde.

salsa verde Process ingredients until finely chopped; season to taste.

do-ahead Salsa verde can be prepared a day ahead; refrigerate in an airtight container.

tips You will need 1 bunch (350g) of watercress. To prepare the watercress, pick off the smaller sprigs and discard the larger thicker stems, which are more peppery.

Salsa verde is such a versatile sauce; it goes well with all meats (steamed and grilled), plus it can be tossed through pasta and used in sandwich fillings. So why not make more than you need, using the whole bunch of each herb, and scaling up the other ingredients. It will keep, refrigerated, for up to 1 week.

Cornichon, French for gherkin, is a very small variety of cucumber. They are available, bottled in a pickled brine, in the condiment section of supermarkets.

TO SAVE MONEY, BUY A CLEANSKIN BOTTLE OF CHARDONNAY, SEMILLON OR RIESLING. CLEANSKINS ARE WINES THAT ARE BOTTLED WITHOUT A WINERY BRANDING OR NAME AND, CONSEQUENTLY, ARE WELL PRICED. THEY ARE SOMETIMES PRODUCED SPECIFICALLY FOR THIS PURPOSE OR MAY BE SURPLUS WINE.

Quick comforting CHICKEN CASSEROLE

PREP & COOK TIME 35 MINUTES   SERVES 4

1 tablespoon olive oil

10 baby new potatoes (400g), halved

2 small red onions (200g), quartered

4 cloves garlic, sliced

8 sprigs fresh thyme

8 chicken thigh cutlets (1.2kg)

2 tablespoons lemon juice

½ cup (125ml) dry white wine

1 cup (250ml) chicken stock

250g (8 ounces) cherry tomatoes

100g (3 ounces) baby spinach leaves

1 tablespoon fresh flat-leaf parsley leaves

crusty bread, to serve

1 Heat oil in a large casserole dish over medium heat. Add potato and onion, cut-sides down; cook for 1½ minutes each side or until browned. Add garlic and thyme; stir for 1 minute or until fragrant; remove vegetables and thyme from pan.
2 Make 3 deep cuts into the skin-side of each cutlet. Heat same pan over high heat; cook chicken, skin-side down, for 2 minutes, turn, cook for a further 2 minutes or until browned. Top with potato mixture.
3 Add lemon juice, wine and stock to pan; season well. Bring to the boil, reduce heat to medium; simmer, covered, for 10 minutes. Add tomatoes; cook for a further 5 minutes or until chicken is cooked through and potato is tender.
4 Remove from heat; stir in spinach. Serve casserole sprinkled with parsley, and accompany with crusty bread to mop up the cooking juices.

One PAN

Paprika and lime
PORK ENCHILADAS

PREP & COOK TIME 30 MINUTES   SERVES 4

1 tablespoon olive oil

500g (1 pound) minced (ground) pork

1 medium red onion (170g), chopped finely

4 cloves garlic, crushed

1 fresh long green chilli, chopped

1 tablespoon smoked paprika

2 x 400g (12½-ounce) canned diced tomatoes

1 tablespoon lime juice

8 x 20cm (8-inch) flour tortillas

2 cups (240g) coarsely grated cheddar

½ cup fresh coriander leaves (cilantro)

4 lime wedges

1 Preheat oven to 220°C/425°F.

2 Heat oil in a large frying pan over high heat. Cook pork, onion, garlic, chilli and paprika, stirring, for 5 minutes or until browned. Add 1 can of tomatoes; cook for 1 minute. Add lime juice; season to taste.

3 Spread tortillas flat on a work surface. Spoon mince mixture equally onto the centre of each tortilla, sprinkle 1 cup cheddar equally over mince mixture; fold tortillas to enclose filling. Place, join-side down, in a single layer, in a 20cm x 30cm (8-inch x 12-inch) shallow ovenproof dish. Spoon over remaining can of tomatoes, leaving the ends of the tortilla exposed, sprinkle with remaining cheddar.

4 Bake for 15 minutes or until golden. Sprinkle enchiladas with coriander; serve with lime wedges.

tip Serve with a simple green or cabbage salad.

YOU CAN ASSEMBLE THE MEATLOAVES AHEAD OF TIME AND REFRIGERATE UNTIL READY TO COOK.

WE USED A 'CLASSIC' SALAD DRESSING AVAILABLE FROM SUPERMARKETS.

Fetta & olive GREEK MEATLOAVES

PREP & COOK TIME 35 MINUTES SERVES 4

500g (1 pound) minced (ground) lamb

1 small red onion (100g), chopped finely

2 tablespoons finely chopped fresh oregano leaves

1 tablespoon finely grated lemon rind

2 cloves garlic, crushed

½ cup (50g) dried breadcrumbs

1 egg

1 medium tomato (150g)

80g (2½ ounces) greek fetta, crumbled

¼ cup (40g) pitted kalamata olives, halved

2 tablespoons olive oil

500g (1 pound) baby new potatoes, quartered

4 cups mesclun salad leaves

1 tablespoon store-bought salad dressing

1 Preheat oven to 220°C/425°F. Lightly grease 4 holes of a 6-hole (¾-cup/180ml) texas muffin pan.

2 Combine mince, onion, oregano, lemon, garlic, breadcrumbs and egg in a large bowl; season. Press half the mixture into the greased pan holes.

3 Cut the tomato into 12 slices. Choose six large tomato slices; place on top of the mince with half the fetta and olives. Top with remaining mince; press mixture down. Top meatloaves with remaining slices of tomato, fetta and olives. Drizzle with 2 teaspoons of the oil.

4 Toss potato and remaining oil in a roasting pan; season.

5 Transfer potato and meatloaves to oven; bake, at the same time, for 20 minutes, or until meatloaves are cooked through. Remove meatloaves from oven. Cook potatoes for a further 5 minutes or until golden.

6 Run a small knife around the edge of each meatloaf; transfer to plates. Drizzle salad leaves with dressing; serve with meatloaves and potato.

Balsamic tomato
AND MUSHROOM CHICKEN

PREP & COOK TIME 30 MINUTES SERVES 4

2 tablespoons olive oil

8 x 125g (4 ounce) chicken thighs

2 cloves garlic, sliced

8 sprigs fresh thyme

4 flat mushrooms (320g), sliced

250g (8 ounces) cherry tomatoes

1 tablespoon balsamic vinegar

80g (2½ ounces) fetta, crumbled

¼ cup coarsely chopped fresh flat-leaf parsley leaves

crusty bread, to serve

1 Heat oil in a large, heavy-based frying pan over high heat. Season chicken; cook, in 2 batches, for 2 minutes each side or until browned. Remove from pan.
2 Reduce heat to medium. Cook garlic, thyme and mushrooms, stirring occasionally, for 5 minutes or until browned. Add tomatoes, cook, stirring, for 1 minute. Return chicken to pan; cook, covered, for 10 minutes or until cooked through.
3 Drizzle chicken with vinegar; sprinkle with fetta and parsley. Serve with bread.

tips Serve with mashed potato instead of bread, if you like. Use skinless chicken thighs, if you prefer.

WE USED A RIESLING-STYLE DRY WINE IN THIS RECIPE. USE ONE RED AND ONE YELLOW CAPSICUM, IF YOU LIKE. THIS DISH WOULD ALSO BE NICE WITH BEEF OR CHICKEN SAUSAGES. SERVE WITH POTATO MASH INSTEAD OF POLENTA.

Sausages & capsicum WITH SOFT POLENTA

PREP & COOK TIME 30 MINUTES **SERVES** 4

2 tablespoons olive oil

6 x 85g (3 ounces) pork and fennel sausages

2 large red capsicums (bell peppers) (700g), sliced thickly

2 large onions (400g), sliced thinly

2 tablespoons fresh rosemary leaves

3 cloves garlic, sliced

1 cup (250ml) dry white wine

1 cup (250ml) chicken stock

250g (8 ounces) green beans, trimmed

5 cups (1.250L) chicken stock, extra

1 cup (170g) polenta

1 cup (80g) finely grated parmesan

30g (1 ounce) butter, chopped

2 tablespoons finely grated parmesan, extra

1 Heat oil in a large, heavy-based frying pan over high heat. Squeeze sausage meat directly from casings, in meatball-sized lumps, into the pan. Cook, turning, for 4 minutes or until browned. Remove from pan.

2 Reduce heat to medium. Cook capsicum, onion, rosemary and garlic for 5 minutes. Add meatballs and wine, cook for 1 minute. Add stock and beans to pan; cook, covered, for 10 minutes or until meatballs are cooked through.

3 Meanwhile, place extra stock in a medium saucepan; bring to the boil. Gradually add polenta. Reduce heat to low; cook, stirring, for 5 minutes or until thickened. Remove from heat, stir in parmesan and butter; season.

4 Serve meatballs with polenta and beans. Sprinkle with extra parmesan.

Couscous and dill CRUSTED SNAPPER

PREP & COOK TIME 20 MINUTES SERVES 4

½ cup (100g) couscous

2 tablespoons coarsely chopped fresh dill

1 clove garlic, crushed

½ cup (125ml) water

2 tablespoons olive oil

4 x 200g (6½ ounce) skinless firm white fish fillets

175g (5½ ounces) broccolini, sliced thickly on the diagonal

2 cups (240g) frozen peas

1 cup (280g) greek-style yoghurt

2 tablespoons tahini (sesame seed paste)

1 tablespoon lemon juice

1 clove garlic, crushed, extra

⅓ cup (25g) flaked almonds, roasted

2 tablespoons coarsely chopped fresh dill, extra

lemon wedges, to serve

1 Preheat oven to 220°C/425°F. Line a large oven tray with baking paper.

2 Place couscous, dill, garlic, water and oil in a small bowl. Using your fingertips, rub couscous grains until evenly covered with mixture; season. Place fish on an oven tray; press couscous mixture onto fish. Bake for 12 minutes or until fish is cooked through and crust is golden.

3 Meanwhile, cook broccolini in a saucepan of boiling water for 2 minutes. Add peas; cook for a further minute or until vegetables are tender, drain.

4 Combine yoghurt, tahini, lemon juice and extra garlic in a small bowl; season. Spoon the yoghurt mixture onto four plates. Top with the vegetables, fish, almonds and extra dill. Serve with lemon wedges.

tip You could also try this with salmon fillets.

TO TEAR HERBS COARSELY, THERE IS NO NEED TO PICK THEM OFF INDIVIDUALLY, SIMPLY USE YOUR HANDS TO TEAR THEM STRAIGHT FROM THE BUNCH. ALTERNATIVELY, RUN A KNIFE OVER THE WHOLE BUNCH, CHOPPING BOTH LEAVES AND STEMS COARSELY. TO CHOP THE NUTS QUICKLY, PULSE BRIEFLY IN THE FOOD PROCESSOR.

Pistachio pilaf
WITH CHAR-GRILLED LAMB

PREP & COOK TIME 35 MINUTES   SERVES 6

30g (1 ounce) butter, chopped

1 medium onion (150g), chopped finely

1 tablespoon finely chopped fresh ginger

1 cinnamon stick

4 cardamom pods, cracked

½ teaspoon ground turmeric

¼ cup loosely packed fresh curry leaves

2 cups (400g) basmati rice

3 cups (750ml) chicken stock or water

12 large french-trimmed lamb cutlets (600g)

2 tablespoons olive oil

2 cups each fresh flat-leaf parsley and mint, torn coarsely

⅓ cup (45g) pistachios, chopped coarsely

⅓ cup (55g) dry-roasted almonds, chopped coarsely

2 tablespoons currants

2 tablespoons lemon juice

lemon wedges and greek-style yoghurt, to serve

1 Heat butter in a large saucepan over medium-high heat, add onion; cook, stirring, for 5 minutes or until softened. Add ginger, spices, curry leaves and rice; stir to combine. Add stock; bring to the boil. Reduce heat to lowest heat; cook, covered, for 10 minutes or until most of the liquid is absorbed. Stand, covered, for 5 minutes.

2 Meanwhile, heat a grill plate (or grill pan or barbecue) to medium-high. Drizzle lamb with oil; season. Cook lamb for 3½ minutes each side for medium, or until cooked to your liking.

3 Stir herbs, nuts, currants and juice into rice pilaf; season to taste. Serve pilaf with cutlets, lemon wedges and yoghurt.

Healthy CHOICE

TO CRUSH THE FENNEL SEEDS, PLACE THEM ON A CHOPPING BOARD AND PRESS DOWN ON THEM WITH THE BASE OF A CLEAN HEAVY-BASED FRYING PAN OR SAUCEPAN. IF YOU CAN FIND PITTED SICILLIAN GREEN OLIVES, USE THEM HERE, OTHERWISE WARN YOUR GUESTS ABOUT THE PITS IN THE OLIVES.

Salami & olive CHICKEN CACCIATORE

PREP & COOK TIME 35 MINUTES SERVES 6

2 teaspoons olive oil

6 x 180g chicken thigh cutlets, skin on

10 baby new potatoes (400g), sliced into thin rounds

130g (4 ounces) sliced salami, chopped coarsely

1 medium brown onion (150g), sliced thinly

6 cloves garlic, crushed

½ teaspoon fennel seeds, crushed

½ cup (125ml) dry white wine

400g (12½ ounces) canned crushed tomatoes

1 cup (250ml) chicken stock

¾ cup (200g) whole sicilian green olives

5 each sprigs fresh thyme and basil

⅓ cup (25g) finely grated parmesan

½ cup fresh small basil leaves, torn

1 Preheat oven to 220°C/425°F.

2 Heat oil in a large casserole over medium-high heat, add chicken, skin-side down; cook for 3 minutes each side or until browned. Remove from pan.

3 Add potato, salami, onion, garlic and fennel to same pan; cook, stirring, for 4 minutes or until onion is golden.

4 Add wine to the pan; stir to combine. Add tomatoes, stock, olives, herb sprigs and chicken; bring to the boil. Transfer to oven; bake, uncovered, for 20 minutes or until chicken is cooked though.

5 Sprinkle cacciatore with parmesan and basil leaves. Served with crusty bread if you like.

Pork & apple sausage
ROLLS WITH CELERY SALAD

Pork & apple sausage ROLLS WITH CELERY SALAD

PREP & COOK TIME 35 MINUTES   SERVES 6

1 green apple (150g), skin on

600g (1¼ pounds) minced (ground) pork and veal mixture

1 cup (60g) finely grated parmesan

1 cup (50g) fine fresh breadcrumbs

1 tablespoon dijon mustard

2 tablespoons fresh thyme, chopped finely

2 eggs, lightly beaten

3 sheets butter puff pastry

1 teaspoon fresh thyme leaves, extra

apple and celery salad

2 tablespoons lemon juice

¼ cup (60ml) extra virgin olive oil

1 tablespoon fresh thyme leaves

2 teaspoons dijon mustard

2 stalks celery with leaves attached (300g), sliced thinly

1 green apple (150g), cut into matchsticks

3 cups watercress sprigs

1 Preheat oven to 220°C/425°F. Grease and line a large oven tray with baking paper.

2 Grate apple; squeeze excess moisture from flesh. Combine mince, parmesan, breadcrumbs, apple, mustard, thyme and half the egg in a medium bowl; season.

3 Place 1 pastry sheet on a work surface. Place a third of the mince mixture in a sausage shape lengthwise 1.5cm (¾-inches) from a long edge. Brush pastry with a little remaining egg; roll to form a sausage roll; trim and discard excess pastry. Repeat with remaining pastry, mince and egg.

4 Place rolls on trays, brush with egg; sprinkle with extra thyme. Bake for 25 minutes or until sausage rolls are golden and cooked through.

5 Meanwhile, make apple and celery salad.

6 Serve salad with sausage rolls.

apple and celery salad Whisk juice, oil, thyme and mustard in a large bowl; season to taste. Add remaining ingredients; toss to combine.

tips A pork and veal mince mixture is available from select supermarkets and butchers. Alternatively buy 300g (9½ ounces) each of pork and veal mince and combine them yourself. You can use all pork mince, if preferred. You will need 1 bunch watercress (350g).

Kid FRIENDLY

Skillet cornbread
WITH BEEF & BEAN CHILLI

PREP & COOK 40 MINUTES   SERVES 6

This recipe is fast to prepare, however the cooking time is a little longer than some of our other recipes. To speed things up, swap the cornbread with rice or tortillas.

1½ tablespoons olive oil

1 medium red onion (170g), sliced thinly

4 cloves garlic, crushed

800g (1½ pounds) minced (ground) beef

1 tablespoon each ground cumin, coriander and smoked paprika

½ teaspoon ground chilli

400g (12½ ounces) canned kidney beans, rinsed, drained

2 cups (500ml) passata (sieved pureed tomato)

½ cup (125ml) chicken stock

1½ tablespoons red wine vinegar

2 tablespoons fresh coriander sprigs (cilantro)

cornbread

1¼ cups (220g) fine instant polenta

¾ cup (110g) self-raising flour

1 teaspoon bicarbonate of soda (baking soda)

1½ cups (375ml) buttermilk

100g (3 ounces) butter, melted

2 eggs

1 cup (140g) corn kernels (see tips)

80g (2½ ounces) fetta, crumbled coarsely

2 green onions (scallions), sliced thinly

1 green chilli, seeded, sliced thinly

1 Make cornbread.

2 Meanwhile, heat oil in a large saucepan over medium-high heat, add onion and garlic; cook, stirring, for 2 minutes or until onion softens. Add mince and spices; cook, breaking mince up with a wooden spoon, for 2 minutes or until browned. Add beans, passata and stock, reduce heat to low; cook for 15 minutes or until mince is cooked through and mixture is thickened slightly. Add vinegar; season to taste.

3 Top chilli with coriander; serve with cornbread, and slices of avocado, if you like.

cornbread Preheat oven to 200°C/400°F. Butter a 25cm (10-inch) top, 18cm (7¼-inch) base, ovenproof frying pan, dust with a little of the polenta. Combine dry ingredients in a large bowl; season. Whisk buttermilk, butter and eggs in a jug. Whisk buttermilk mixture into dry ingredients; stir in corn, fetta, onion and chilli. Pour into frying pan; bake for 20 minutes or until golden and cooked through.

tips We made this beef & bean chilli a mild 'family friendly' dish, meaning there is only a hint of chilli for any children, or adults, who don't like the heat. If you want a bit of a chilli kick, feel free to add more.
You can use fresh, frozen or canned corn kernels for the cornbread. You could also make the cornbread in a 22cm (9-inch) springform pan instead of a frying pan (skillet). The chilli and cornbread can be made a day ahead and reheated, or can be frozen for up to 1 month. You could also serve the chilli topped with 1 coarsely chopped medium avocado, sour cream and lime wedges.

Pork & bean sprout SINGAPORE NOODLES

PREP & COOK TIME 30 MINUTES   SERVES 4

300g (9½ ounces) dried rice vermicelli noodles

2 tablespoons mild curry powder

1 tablespoon dark soy sauce

2 tablespoons chinese cooking wine (shaoxing)

2 teaspoons white (granulated) sugar

½ cup (125ml) water

¼ cup (60ml) vegetable oil

1 medium red onion (170g), halved, sliced thinly

1 medium red capsicum (bell pepper) (200g), seeded, sliced thickly

3 cups (240g) shredded green cabbage

2½ cups (200g) bean sprouts

300g (9½ ounces) chinese barbecued pork, sliced thinly

1 cup loosely packed fresh coriander (cilantro) leaves

½ cup (40g) bean sprouts, extra

1 Soak noodles in a large bowl of cold water for 8 minutes or until softened. Drain.

2 Meanwhile, stir curry powder, sauce, cooking wine, sugar and the water in a small bowl until sugar dissolves.

3 Heat 1 tablespoon of the oil in a wok over medium-high heat. Add onion; stir-fry for 1 minute. Add capsicum; stir-fry for a further minute. Add cabbage; stir-fry for 2 minutes or until softened slightly. Remove vegetables from wok.

4 Heat remaining oil in wok over medium heat. Add curry powder mixture; stir-fry for 5 minutes. Add noodles; toss well to coat in spice mixture. Add remaining ingredients except coriander; stir-fry for 1 minute or until heated through and well combined.

5 Divide noodle mixture among bowls; served topped with coriander and extra bean sprouts.

tip You could use a barbecue chicken or cooked shelled prawns in place of the pork.

Sichuan MA PO TOFU

PREP & COOK TIME 25 MINUTES SERVES 4

This recipe hails from the Sichuan region of China, an area renowned for its love of chilli. The name is derived from the words 'ma' meaning disfigured person and 'po' meaning old woman, a reference to the old pockmarked woman who is said to have created it.

2 teaspoons sichuan peppercorns, toasted, lightly crushed

1 tablespoon cornflour

¼ cup (60ml) chinese cooking wine (shaoxing)

1 cup (250ml) chicken stock

2 teaspoons light soy sauce

3 teaspoons white (granulated) sugar

½ cup (125ml) water

1 tablespoon sesame oil

4 cloves garlic, crushed

300g (9½ ounces) minced (ground) pork

2 tablespoons chilli bean paste (see tips)

300g (9½ ounces) fresh silken tofu, drained, cut into 2cm (¾-inch) cubes

¼ cup (35g) roasted peanuts, coarsely chopped

2 green onions (scallions), sliced thinly

1 Stir peppercorns in a wok over medium heat for 1 minute or until fragrant. Crush lightly with a pestle and mortar. (Alternatively, place on a chopping board and crush with the base of a clean, heavy-based saucepan.)

2 Whisk cornflour, cooking wine, stock, sauce, sugar and the water in a medium jug until combined.

3 Heat sesame oil in a wok over high heat. Add garlic and pork; stir-fry for 8 minutes or until pork is browned. Stir in bean paste and half the peppercorns; stir-fry mixture for a further minute.

4 Stir cornflour mixture into pork mixture in wok; cook until mixture boils and thickens slightly. Reduce heat to medium; cook for 5 minutes. Carefully add tofu and stir gently to combine. Cook for a further 2 minutes or until heated through.

5 Divide ma po tofu among bowls; top with peanuts, onion and remaining crushed peppercorns. Serve with steamed rice, if you like.

Crisp-skinned ginger
FISH WITH COCONUT RICE

PREP & COOK TIME 30 MINUTES   SERVES 4

½ cup (40g) shredded coconut, toasted

vegetable oil, for frying

50g (1½-ounce) piece fresh ginger, peeled, cut into matchsticks

4 x 200g (6½-ounce) snapper fillets

1 green onion (scallion)

1 teaspoon finely grated fresh ginger

⅓ cup (80ml) lime juice

⅓ cup (80ml) water

1 tablespoon fish sauce

1 small fresh red thai (serrano) chilli, sliced thinly

1 tablespoon caster (superfine) sugar

coconut rice

1½ cups (300g) jasmine rice, rinsed, drained

270ml canned coconut milk

⅔ cup (160ml) water

2 teaspoons finely grated fresh ginger

1 Make coconut rice.

2 Dry-fry coconut in a large frying pan, over medium heat, stirring constantly, until golden. Remove immediately from pan.

3 Pour enough oil into a large frying pan to cover base. Heat over medium heat; stir-fry ginger strips for 1 minute or until golden. Remove with a slotted spoon; drain on paper towel. Combine ginger and coconut in a small bowl.

4 Carefully pour out oil leaving 2 tablespoons in the pan. Increase heat to medium-high. Season fish on both sides with salt. Cook fish, skin-side down, for 3 minutes or until golden and crisp; turn fish over, cook for a further minute or until just cooked through.

5 Slice half the green onion on the diagonal; finely chop the remaining half.

6 To make dipping sauce, stir grated ginger, juice, the water, sauce, chilli, finely chopped green onion and sugar in a small bowl until sugar dissolves.

7 Top fish with crisp ginger mixture and remaining onion. Serve with coconut rice and ginger dipping sauce.

coconut rice Place rice, coconut milk, the water and ginger in a saucepan, season with salt; stir well to combine. Cover pan with a lid; bring to the boil over medium heat. Reduce to lowest heat; cook for 10 minutes. Turn off the heat; stand, covered, for a further 5 minutes before removing lid.

tips You could use chicken instead of fish. Serve with asian greens such as gai lan.

Portuguese
PIRI PIRI CHICKEN

PREP & COOK TIME 35 MINUTES · SERVES 4

While some families are happy to eat hot and spicy meals, this recipe may be a little hot for younger, and older, children who aren't specifically used to a kick of chilli in their food (this is also true for adults). If you and your family are not used to hot and spicy tastes, try reducing the amount of chilli in the piri piri sauce, adding only enough to suit your heat tolerance.

2 medium desiree potatoes (400g)

1.4kg (2¾-pound) butterflied chicken

⅓ cup (80ml) vegetable oil

piri piri sauce

6 fresh long red chillies

1 teaspoon finely grated lemon rind

2 tablespoons lemon juice

4 cloves garlic, halved

2 teaspoons sweet paprika

¼ cup coarsely chopped fresh oregano

½ cup (125ml) olive oil

1 Preheat oven to 200°C/400°F.

2 Make piri piri sauce.

3 Prick potatoes all over with a fork. Microwave on HIGH (100%) for 3 minutes or until potatoes are tender. Cut into 4cm (1½-inch) pieces.

4 Meanwhile, rub ⅓ cup piri piri sauce over both sides of chicken. Heat oil in a large flameproof roasting pan over medium-high heat. Cook chicken, skin-side down, for 5 minutes. Turn chicken over. Add potato to pan; cook a further 5 minutes, turning potato until golden. Transfer pan to oven; roast chicken for 15 minutes or until juices run clear when the thickest part of a thigh is pierced.

5 Place potato and chicken on a platter. Serve with piri piri sauce, and a green salad, if you like.

piri piri sauce Discard seeds from 3 chillies, then coarsely chop all the chillies; process with remaining ingredients until well combined. Season well with salt.

tips Ask the butcher to butterfly the chicken for you. Or, to do it yourself, use a large heavy, flat-bladed knife or kitchen scissors to cut along each side of the backbone; discard bone. Open chicken out and press down on the breast bone to flatten. You can use other cuts of chicken on the bone, such as wings, cutlets and marylands.

Butter miso
MUSHROOM RISOTTO

PREP & COOK TIME 35 MINUTES **SERVES** 4

This risotto is made using a rice cooker.

2 green onions (scallions)

1½ cups (300g) sushi rice

30g (1 ounce) butter

200g (6½ ounces) oyster mushrooms, sliced

200g (6½ ounces) shiitake mushrooms, sliced

1 tablespoon sesame oil

3 cups (750ml) boiling water

½ cup (130g) shiro (white) miso paste

¼ cup (60ml) water, extra

2 cups baby spinach leaves

30g (1 ounce) butter, extra

2 teaspoons sesame seeds

1 Thinly slice green onions, keep white and green parts separate.

2 Rinse rice under running water until water runs clear.

3 Set rice cooker to sauté or regular cook function; add butter. Once melted, cook mushrooms and white part of onion for 5 minutes or until softened. Season; remove from cooker.

4 Add 1 tablespoon sesame oil to the cooker. Once hot, add rinsed rice, stir to coat in oil. Pour the water into rice cooker. Cook, covered, on risotto setting for 10 minutes.

5 Stir mushroom mixture into cooker, cover; cook until cooker function changes to warm. Whisk miso paste and the extra water together. Add to cooker with spinach and extra butter, stir until spinach wilts and butter melts. Season.

6 Divide risotto among bowls; sprinkle with sesame seeds and remaining green onion.

Moroccan-style CHICKEN WITH QUINOA

PREP & COOK TIME 35 MINUTES   SERVES 4

1½ cups (300g) tri-coloured quinoa

3 cups (750ml) boiling water

1 tablespoon finely chopped preserved lemon rind

pinch saffron threads

2 cloves garlic, crushed

1 medium red onion (170g), chopped finely

1 teaspoon ground ginger

1 cinnamon stick

¼ teaspoon salt

1 whole barbecued chicken

¼ cup (40g) pine nuts, toasted

⅔ cup (80g) pitted sicilian green olives

½ cup coarsely chopped fresh coriander (cilantro)

½ cup coarsely chopped fresh flat-leaf parsley

2 tablespoons lemon juice

¼ cup (60ml) extra virgin olive oil

1 Rinse quinoa in a fine sieve under running water; drain well.

2 Place quinoa, the boiling water, preserved lemon rind, saffron, garlic, onion, ginger, cinnamon and salt into a rice cooker; stir to combine. Set cooker to regular cook function; cook, covered, for 15 minutes.

3 Meanwhile, shred chicken meat from chicken in large pieces; discard skin and bones. Add chicken to cooker; cook, covered, for a further 10 minutes or until quinoa is tender and chicken is heated through.

4 Transfer quinoa mixture to a large serving bowl; combine with nuts, olives, herbs, lemon juice and olive oil. Season to taste.

Rice-cooker *BIBIMBAP*

PREP & COOK TIME 35 MINUTES SERVES 4

Bibimbap is a popular every-day Korean dish of rice, topped with vegetables, meat and a raw egg; it is designed to be mixed together at the last moment to combine all the flavours. Our recipe is speedily made in a rice cooker.

2 cups (400g) sushi rice

1½ tablespoons sesame oil

1 medium carrot (120g), cut into matchsticks

1 medium zucchini (120g), cut into matchsticks

250g (8 ounces) minced (ground) beef

1 clove garlic, crushed

1 tablespoon light soy sauce

1 teaspoon caster (superfine) sugar

1 clove garlic, crushed, extra

1 cup (260g) kimchi, chopped

2 cups (500ml) boiling water

½ cup bean sprouts

3 egg yolks

½ teaspoon sesame oil, extra

1 Rinse rice under running water until water runs clear.

2 Set rice cooker to sauté or regular cook function. Add 2 teaspoons of the oil to cooker; cook carrot and zucchini, stirring, for 2 minutes or until slightly softened. Remove from cooker.

3 Heat another 2 teaspoons of oil in cooker; cook beef and garlic, stirring, for 5 minutes or until browned. Stir in sauce and sugar; remove from cooker, cover to keep warm.

4 Place another 2 teaspoons of the oil, rice, extra garlic, half of the kimchi and the boiling water in the cooker; stir to combine then close lid. Set to regular cook function.

5 In the last 5 minutes of the cooking time, top the kimchi mixture with zucchini, carrot, beef, bean sprouts and remaining kimchi, keeping each ingredient separate.

6 To serve, place the egg yolks into the centre of the bibimbap and stir to combine; drizzle with the extra oil.

tip Kimchi is a spicy fermented cabbage used in Korean cooking and as a condiment; it is available from Asian food stores and some delis.

Italian sausages
WITH BEANS AND CRUMBS

PREP & COOK TIME 35 MINUTES   SERVES 4

¼ cup (60ml) olive oil

500g (1 pound) italian pork and fennel sausages

1 medium red onion (170g), chopped coarsely

¼ teaspoon dried chilli flakes

2 teaspoons smoked paprika

400g (12½ ounces) canned cherry or chopped tomatoes

1½ cups (375ml) chicken stock

1 tablespoon fresh thyme leaves

2 x 400g (12½-ounce) cans butter beans, rinsed, drained

250g (8-ounce) piece sourdough bread, coarsely torn into breadcrumbs

¼ cup fresh flat-leaf parsley leaves

1 Heat 1 tablespoon of the oil in a medium saucepan over medium-high heat. Squeeze sausage meat out of the casings into rough meatball-sized pieces, directly into the pan. Add onion, cook, stirring frequently, for 8 minutes or until sausage meat is browned.

2 Add chilli, paprika, tomatoes, stock and thyme to pan; stir to combine. Cook, partially covered, for 10 minutes or until mixture thickens slightly. Add beans; cook, uncovered, for a further 5 minutes or until heated through.

3 Meanwhile, heat remaining oil in a small frying pan over medium heat. Add breadcrumbs, cook, stirring, for 8 minutes or until golden. Season to taste.

4 Divide sausage mixture among bowls; top with breadcrumbs and parsley.

tip You can use any kind of canned beans for this recipe.

EXPRESS DESSERTS

PEANUT BRITTLE IS AVAILABLE FROM MAJOR SUPERMARKETS AND CONFECTIONERY STORES. IF YOU DON'T HAVE A PIPING BAG, SIMPLY USE A ZIPTOP BAG; FILL BAG WITH CREAM MIXTURE, TWIST AND SNIP A 1CM (½-INCH) HOLE FROM ONE CORNER. FOR A MORE TRADITIONAL FILLING, PROCESS 150G (4½ OUNCES) RICOTTA UNTIL SMOOTH. WHIP ½ CUP POURING CREAM TO SOFT PEAKS; FOLD THE CREAM AND RICOTTA THROUGH THE BRITTLE.

Peanut BRITTLE CANNOLI

PREP & COOK TIME 15 MINUTES   SERVES 6

2 teaspoons vanilla extract

300ml thickened (heavy) cream

200g (6½ ounces) chocolate-coated peanut brittle, chopped finely

12 store-bought cannoli shells (150g)

icing (confectioners') sugar, for dusting

chocolate sauce

300ml pouring cream

100g (3 ounces) dark chocolate, chopped coarsely

1 Make chocolate sauce.

2 Beat vanilla and cream in a small bowl with an electric mixer until firm peaks form; stir in 150g (4½ ounces) of the brittle.

3 Fit a large piping bag with a large plain nozzle; fill with brittle cream. Pipe filling into cannoli shells; dust with sifted icing sugar. Serve cannoli with chocolate sauce and remaining brittle.

chocolate sauce Heat cream in a small saucepan until almost boiling; remove from heat. Add chocolate, whisk until smooth.

Healthy CHOICE

YOU NEED 4 PASSIONFRUIT FOR THIS RECIPE. MERINGUE NESTS
AND LEMON CURD ARE AVAILABLE FROM MAJOR SUPERMARKETS.

Lemon & meringue
PASSIONFRUIT MESS

PREP TIME 15 MINUTES **SERVES** 8

300ml thickened (heavy) cream

2 tablespoons icing (confectioners') sugar

1 cup (280g) greek-style yoghurt

8 store-bought meringue nests (80g), crushed coarsely

⅔ cup (200ml) lemon curd

⅓ cup (80g) passionfruit pulp

⅓ cup (15g) flaked coconut, toasted

125g (4 ounces) fresh raspberries

1 Beat cream and sugar in a small bowl with an electric mixer until firm peaks form; gently fold in yoghurt.
2 Arrange half the meringue over a platter. Spoon cream mixture over meringue; drop spoonfuls of curd over cream. Using a small knife, swirl curd through cream.
3 Top with remaining meringue, passionfruit, coconut and raspberries.

Cherry
HAZELNUT CAKE

MAKE SURE TO WARN EATERS THAT THE CHERRIES CONTAIN PIPS. IF YOU LIKE, YOU COULD ADD 1 TEASPOON OF EITHER FINELY GRATED LEMON OR ORANGE RIND WHEN BEATING THE BUTTER AND SUGAR IN STEP 2. GROUND ALMONDS CAN ALSO BE USED IN PLACE OF GROUND HAZELNUTS, IF YOU PREFER.

Cherry
HAZELNUT CAKE

PREP & COOK TIME 30 MINUTES (& STANDING) SERVES 8

150g (4½ ounces) butter, softened

⅔ cup (150g) caster (superfine) sugar

2 eggs

½ cup (75g) plain (all-purpose) flour

1½ cups (180g) ground hazelnuts

16 fresh cherries (150g), stalks attached

icing (confectioners') sugar, for dusting

¾ cup (180ml) thick (double) cream

⅓ cup (80ml) maple syrup

1 Preheat oven to 200°C/400°F. Grease a 19cm (7¾-inch) square cake pan; line base and sides with baking paper, extending paper 5cm (2-inches) above edges.
2 Beat butter and sugar in a small bowl with an electric mixer until pale and fluffy. Add eggs, beat until just combined, then add sifted flour and hazelnuts; beat on low speed until just combined.
3 Spread mixture evenly into pan; bake for 10 minutes.
4 Top cake with cherries, gently pushing them a quarter of the way into the cake mix. Bake cake for a further 10 minutes or until a skewer inserted into the centre comes out clean. Stand cake in pan for 3 minutes before turning, top-side up, onto a board. Dust with sifted icing sugar. Serve cake warm with cream and maple syrup.

YOU COULD USE PEARS INSTEAD OF APPLES. USE A FIRM VARIETY THAT
HOLDS ITS SHAPE DURING COOKING, SUCH AS PACKHAM OR BEURRE BOSC.

Salted caramel & apple
ICE-CREAM SUNDAES

PREP & COOK TIME 10 MINUTES   SERVES 4

80g (2½ ounces) butter, chopped

2 large apples (400g), peeled, chopped coarsely

1 tablespoon lemon juice

½ cup (75g) brown sugar

¼ teaspoon mixed spice

¼ teaspoon sea salt flakes

¼ cup (60ml) pouring cream

8 scoops vanilla ice-cream

4 amaretti biscuits, crumbled

¼ cup (40g) toasted pine nuts

1 Melt butter in a large frying pan over medium heat. Add apples and lemon juice; cook for 5 minutes. Add sugar, spice, salt and cream; cook, stirring, for 1 minute.
2 Divide ice-cream among glasses. Spoon over warm apple mixture; sprinkle with biscuits and pine nuts. Serve sundaes immediately.

Cheap
EAT

Spanish caramel ORANGE CAKE

ORANGE CAKE

PREP & COOK TIME 25 MINUTES SERVES 8

2 tablespoons caster (superfine) sugar

1 tablespoon lemon juice

¾ cup (180ml) strained orange juice

250g (8 ounces) mascarpone

1 cup (310g) dulce de leche

2 good-quality store-bought round unfilled sponge cakes (460g)

4 medium blood oranges (960g), peeled, sliced thinly

¼ cup (20g) flaked almonds, roasted

1 Place sugar and juices in a medium saucepan; stir over medium heat until sugar dissolves. Bring to the boil; boil for 5 minutes or until thickens slightly and reduces to ⅓ cup. Transfer syrup to a small jug; cool quickly by placing in a bowl of iced water for 10 minutes.
2 Meanwhile, whisk mascarpone and dulce de leche in a medium bowl until soft peaks form.
3 Split each cake in half horizontally so you have 4 layers.
4 Place one cake layer, cut-side up, on a cake plate. Brush with 1 tablespoon of the cooled syrup. Spread with one quarter of the dulce de leche cream. Repeat layers three more times with remaining cake, syrup and dulce de leche cream. Top cake with half the sliced oranges and sprinkle with almonds. Serve cake accompanied with remaining orange slices.

tip Dulce de leche is a caramel spread originating in South America. It is made by simmering sweetened milk until thick and caramelised. It is available in jars from delis. You can substitute Caramel Top 'n' Fill from supermarkets.

WE USED A BOTTLED PANCAKE MIXTURE DESIGNED TO BE MIXED AND SHAKEN IN THE BOTTLE. ANY LEFTOVER PANCAKE BATTER CAN BE STORED IN THE FRIDGE AND USED THE FOLLOWING DAY.

Pear fritters with
RASPBERRY ROSE SYRUP

PREP & COOK TIME 20 MINUTES   SERVES 4

200g (6½-ounce) bottle pancake shake mixture (see tip)

¼ cup (60ml) vegetable oil

2 medium firm pears (460g), peeled, cored, sliced thickly

2 tablespoons fresh raspberries

⅓ cup (115g) honey

1 teaspoon rosewater

⅓ cup (95g) greek-style yoghurt

2 tablespoons coarsely chopped raw pistachios

fresh raspberries, extra, to serve

1 Make pancake batter according to bottle instructions. Pour into a small bowl.

2 Heat 1 tablespoon of the oil in a large frying pan over medium heat.

3 Add pear slices to the pancake batter. Cook coated pear slices, in batches, adding more oil in between, for 2 minutes each side or until golden. Drain on kitchen paper.

4 Place raspberries, honey and rosewater in a small bowl; mash with a fork to combine and crush.

5 Divide fritters among bowls. Top with yoghurt and raspberry rose syrup. Sprinkle with pistachios.

Apple & cinnamon
HAND PIES

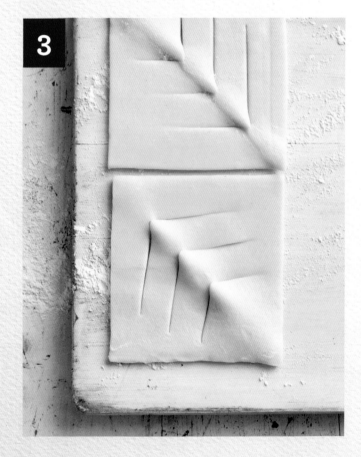

Apple & cinnamon HAND PIES

PREP & COOK TIME 40 MINUTES MAKES 4

400g (12½ ounces) canned sliced pie apple

pinch each of ground cloves, nutmeg and ginger

¼ teaspoon ground cinnamon

1½ tablespoons caster (superfine) sugar

1 teaspoon finely grated lemon rind

2 sheets puff pastry

1 egg yolk

1 teaspoon water

icing (confectioners') sugar, to dust

vanilla ice-cream, to serve

1 Preheat oven to 220°C/425°F. Line an oven tray with baking paper.

2 Combine apple, spices, sugar and rind in a medium bowl.

3 Cut each pastry sheet into four squares; spoon apple mixture over four squares, leaving a 2cm (¾-inch) border around edges. Brush pastry edges with combined egg yolk and the water.

4 Gently fold remaining pastry squares in half diagonally to form triangles.

5 Using a floured knife, make four small diagonal cuts, 2cm (¾-inch) apart, along folded pastry edge. Open pastry out to form squares again.

6 Place a decorated pastry square over an apple base; press down edges to seal, trim. Repeat with remaining pastry squares and bases, brush with remaining egg yolk.

7 Bake pies for 25 minutes or until browned and crisp.

8 Dust with icing sugar. Serve pies warm with ice-cream.

do-ahead Unbaked pies can be prepared several hours ahead; refrigerate, covered.

Vanilla & hazelnut
STRAWBERRY GALETTE

PREP & COOK TIME 35 MINUTES SERVES 8

2 sheets shortcrust pastry

¾ cup (180g) firm fresh ricotta

⅓ cup (75g) caster (superfine) sugar

1 teaspoon vanilla extract

1 egg, lightly beaten

500g (1 pound) strawberries

¼ cup (25g) ground hazelnuts

1 teaspoon cornflour (cornstarch)

2 teaspoons finely grated orange rind

1 tablespoon icing (confectioners') sugar

greek-style yoghurt, to serve

1 Grease and line a large oven tray. Place tray in oven. Preheat oven with tray to 200°C/400°F.

2 Cut a pastry sheet in half. Place pastry halves along the top and side of the second pastry sheet on a piece of baking paper; press joins to form one large sheet of pastry. Roll out pastry slightly into a 30cm (12-inch) square. Using a plate or bowl as a guide, mark, don't cut, a 26cm (10½-inch) round in the centre of the pastry. Trim corners of pastry slightly.

3 Combine ricotta, 1 tablespoon of caster sugar and vanilla in a small bowl; spread inside marked circle. Brush pastry border with beaten egg; roll pastry border up towards filling. Bake tart for 25 minutes, covering with greased foil if it starts to overbrown.

4 Meanwhile, thinly slice strawberries. Place remaining caster sugar, hazelnuts, cornflour and rind in a bowl; stir to combine. Just before removing tart from oven, add strawberry slices to hazelnut mixture; toss gently to combine.

5 Working quickly, remove tart from oven; sprinkle strawberry mixture evenly over ricotta layer; bake tart for a further 5 minutes or until pastry is golden and strawberries are warmed through.

6 Dust tart with sifted icing sugar; serve immediately, accompanied with yoghurt.

WE USED A 900-WATT MICROWAVE OVEN. IF YOUR MICROWAVE OVEN IS A DIFFERENT WATTAGE YOU MAY NEED TO ADJUST THE COOKING TIME OF THE PUDDINGS. YOU COULD ALSO SERVE THE PUDDINGS TOPPED WITH CHOPPED TOASTED HAZELNUTS.

Chocolate Nutella
MUG PUDDINGS

PREP & COOK TIME 5 MINUTES   SERVES 4

1 cup (150g) self-raising flour

½ cup (110g) brown sugar

½ cup (50g) cocoa powder

2 eggs

1 cup (250ml) milk

½ cup (125ml) vegetable oil

½ cup (165g) Nutella

4 scoops chocolate ice-cream

1 Combine flour, sugar and cocoa in a small bowl. Add egg, milk and oil; whisk to combine. Pour mixture into 4 x 1½-cup (375ml) microwave-safe mugs. (Make sure you use the right sized mugs or the mixture will overflow). Drop 1½ tablespoons Nutella into each mug.

2 Microwave on MEDIUM for 1½ minutes or until cooked but slightly gooey at the bottom. Serve immediately topped with ice-cream.

Waffles with MARMALADE RICOTTA

250g (8 ounces) ricotta

¼ cup (85g) orange marmalade

2 tablespoons milk

2 tablespoons caster (superfine) sugar

4 store-bought waffles (360g), warmed

250g (8 ounces) strawberries, chopped coarsely

3 teaspoons finely grated orange rind

icing (confectioners') sugar, to dust

1 Process ricotta, marmalade, milk and sugar until smooth and fluffy.

2 Toast waffles in a toaster. Place on serving plates; top with ricotta mixture and strawberries. Sprinkle with orange rind and dust with sifted icing sugar to serve.

tips You can make the whipped ricotta ahead of time; cover and refrigerate. Change the flavour of the whipped ricotta by varying the marmalade; you could try lime, ginger or cumquat marmalade.

Baklava & berry
TURKISH DELIGHT TRIFLES

PREP TIME 10 MINUTES   SERVES 2

200g (6 ½ ounces) baklava, chopped coarsely

1½ cups (420g) greek-style yoghurt

60g (2 ounces) turkish delight, chopped coarsely

100g (3 ounces) strawberries, chopped coarsely

60g (2 ounces) raspberries

2 tablespoons chopped walnuts, roasted

icing (confectioners') sugar, for dusting

1 Divide half the baklava between the bases of two 2-cup glasses. Top with half of the yoghurt, turkish delight, berries then remaining baklava. Repeat with remaining yoghurt, turkish delight and berries. Sprinkle with walnuts; dust with icing sugar to serve.

tips To stop the turkish delight sticking to your knife when cutting it, first spray the knife with cooking-oil spray. You could also use kourabiethe (Greek shortbread) instead of baklava, which is available from most major supermarkets.

PEAR POACHING LIQUID CAN BE USED IN SMOOTHIES AND TO SOAK OATS FOR BIRCHER MUESLI OR TO MOISTEN CAKES. YOU COULD SERVE THIS PUDDING WITH VANILLA ICE-CREAM.

Coconut rice pudding
& POACHED PEARS

PREP & COOK TIME 30 MINUTES **SERVES** 4

2 cups (500ml) clear apple juice

1 cinnamon stick

2 medium pears (460g), peeled, quartered lengthways

500g (1-pound) packet 90-second microwave brown rice

1½ cups (375ml) light coconut milk

⅓ cup (75g) firmly packed brown sugar

1 teaspoon ground cinnamon

1 teaspoon vanilla bean paste

2 tablespoons honey

⅓ cup (55g) dried apricots, chopped finely

1 cup (280g) greek-style yoghurt

1 Place juice and cinnamon stick in a small saucepan. Bring to the boil. Add pears, reduce heat to medium; cook for 10 minutes or until fruit is just tender. Remove pears from pan; reserve cooking liquid for another use (see tips), discard cinnamon stick.

2 Combine rice, coconut milk, ¼ cup of the sugar, ground cinnamon and vanilla paste in a medium saucepan. Bring to a simmer; simmer over low heat, stirring, for 5 minutes or until heated through.

3 Meanwhile, combine honey and remaining 2 tablespoons sugar in a small frying pan over medium heat, stirring until sugar dissolves. Add apricot; cook, stirring, for 2 minutes or until coated and heated through.

4 Divide rice pudding among bowls; top with pears, yoghurt and apricot mixture.

Cheap
EAT

YOU CAN ASSEMBLE THE ICE-CREAM SANDWICHES UP TO

A DAY AHEAD AND STORE, COVERED, IN THE FREEZER.

Peanut and honey ICE-CREAM SANDWICHES

PREP TIME 15 MINUTES   SERVES 4

8 digestive biscuits (120g)

1 cup vanilla ice-cream, softened slightly

1 small banana (130g), sliced thinly

¼ cup (70g) crunchy peanut butter

1 tablespoon honey

⅔ cup (90g) chopped salted, roasted peanuts

1 Line an oven tray with baking paper. Place 4 biscuits on the tray. Working quickly, place an egg ring on top of a biscuit and fill with ¼ cup of the ice-cream. Repeat with remaining 3 biscuits and ice-cream; carefully remove egg rings. Top the ice-cream with banana; place in the freezer.

2 Meanwhile, combine peanut butter and honey in a small bowl; spread the remaining 4 biscuits with peanut butter mixture. Place biscuits, peanut butter-side down, on top of ice-cream and banana to sandwich. Roll the edges in the chopped peanuts. Freeze for 10 minutes or until firm.

Microwave
FRUIT SALADS

Watermelon & LYCHEE

PREP & COOK 20 MINUTES   SERVES 8

Cut 1.5kg (3lb) seedless watermelon into small wedges. Peel and seed 16 fresh lychees. Place in a large bowl with 150g (4½oz) raspberries. Combine 1½ cups caster (superfine) sugar and 1½ cups water in a medium microwave safe bowl; microwave on HIGH (100%) for 3 minutes or until sugar dissolves and syrup is hot. Cut a 4cm (1½-inch) piece ginger into matchsticks. Carefully remove bowl from the microwave; add ¼ cup lime juice, 2 teaspoons finely grated lime rind, 1 teaspoon vanilla bean paste and the ginger. Cool mixture over a bowl of ice. Pour syrup mixture over fruit mixture. Beat 1 cup each cream and greek-style yoghurt in a small bowl with an electric mixer until soft peaks form. Serve fruit salad with yoghurt cream, sprinkle with 2 teaspoons toasted white sesame seeds.

Blood orange & ROSEMARY

PREP & COOK TIME 15 MINUTES   SERVES 4

Remove rind from 1 blood orange in long thin strips with a zesting tool; reserve rind and orange. Peel and discard rind and pith from 5 more blood oranges. Cut all oranges crossways into rounds. Combine reserved orange rind strips, 1 cup caster (superfine) sugar, ½ cup water and 2 small rosemary sprigs in a large microwave safe bowl; microwave on HIGH (100%) for 2½ minutes or until sugar dissolves and syrup is hot. Add orange slices and 2 tablespoons lemon juice. Stand for 10 minutes or until cooled slightly. Divide fruit salad among bowls; top with 2 tablespoons crumbled pistachio halva, if desired.

tip Halva is a confectionery made from ground sesame seeds and sugar; it is available from Middle Eastern stores.

Cherry & LEMONADE

PREP & COOK TIME 20 MINUTES **SERVES** 4

Pit 225g (7oz) fresh cherries; place in a large microwave safe bowl with 1 cup lemonade. Microwave on HIGH (100%) for 2 minutes or until cherries soften slightly, mashing fruit slightly with a fork half way through cooking time. Slice 500g (1lb) strawberries into rounds. Toss strawberries and 1½ teaspoons grated lemon rind with warm cherry mixture; spoon fruit salad into four serving glasses. Pour an extra ⅔ cup chilled lemonade equally among glasses. Top each glass with a scoop of lemon sorbet. Serve immediately.

Mango, chilli & KAFFIR LIME

PREP & COOK TIME 20 MINUTES **SERVES** 4

Remove cheeks from 4 medium chilled mangoes. Using a large kitchen spoon, scoop between flesh and skin to remove the cheek flesh in one piece. Slice flesh lengthwise into wedges; place in a large bowl. Grate 125g (4oz) palm sugar into a small microwave safe bowl; add ½ cup water and 6 crushed fresh kaffir lime leaves; microwave on HIGH (100%) for 1½ minutes or until sugar dissolves. Add ½ finely chopped seeded fresh long chilli, 1 teaspoon finely grated lime rind and ¼ cup lime juice. Pour hot syrup mixture over mango; toss to combine. Serve topped with ½ cup flaked coconut.

Dutch chocolate
PANCAKES WITH BANANA

PANCAKES WITH BANANA

PREP & COOK TIME 25 MINUTES   SERVES 4

¾ cup (180ml) milk

⅔ cup (100g) plain (all-purpose) flour

4 eggs

2 tablespoons dutch-processed cocoa

½ cup (110g) caster (superfine) sugar

1 teaspoon vanilla bean paste

100g (3 ounces) dark (bittersweet) chocolate, chopped coarsely

30g (1 ounce) butter

2 small bananas (260g), halved lengthways and crossways

4 scoops chocolate or chocolate chip ice-cream

1 teaspoon dutch-processed cocoa, extra

1 Preheat oven to 200°C/400°F.

2 Pulse milk, flour, eggs, cocoa, sugar, vanilla and a pinch of salt in a food processor for 15 seconds or until just combined (do not over process or the mixture will be tough). Stir in half the chocolate.

3 Heat butter in an 18cm (7¼-inch) base and 25cm (10-inch) top, ovenproof frying pan, over medium heat, for 1 minute or until foaming; add batter. Immediately transfer to the oven; bake for 12 minutes or until puffed and cooked through.

4 Gently melt remaining chocolate in a microwave or a small heatproof bowl over a saucepan of simmering water.

5 Top pancake with bananas and ice-cream, drizzle with melted chocolate and dust with extra sifted cocoa; serve pancake immediately.

Date & carrot
BUTTERSCOTCH PUDDINGS

Date & carrot
BUTTERSCOTCH PUDDINGS

BUTTERSCOTCH PUDDINGS

PREP & COOK TIME 35 MINUTES   SERVES 8

16 fresh medjool dates (200g), pitted

⅔ cup (160ml) boiling water

1 teaspoon bicarbonate of soda (baking soda)

1 small carrot (70g), chopped coarsely

¼ cup (30g) pecans

90g (3 ounces) butter, chopped, softened

2 eggs

¾ cup (165g) firmly packed brown sugar

1¼ cups (185g) self-raising flour

1 teaspoon ground cinnamon

1 teaspoon vanilla bean paste

⅓ cup (40g) pecans, extra

butterscotch sauce

125g (4 ounces) butter, chopped coarsely

½ cup (110g) firmly packed brown sugar

½ cup (125ml) double (heavy) cream

1 teaspoons fine sea salt

1 Preheat oven to 180°C/350°F. Grease an 8-hole, ¾-cup (180ml) mini loaf pan tray.

2 Combine dates, the boiling water and soda in a small bowl; stand for 5 minutes.

3 Process carrot and pecans until finely chopped. Add dates and soaking liquid; pulse to combine. Add butter, eggs, sugar, flour, cinnamon and vanilla; pulse to combine.

4 Spoon mixture into holes; sprinkle tops with extra pecans. bake for 15 minutes or until a skewer inserted into the centre comes out clean. Stand cakes in pans for 5 minutes before turning, top-side up, onto a wire rack.

5 Meanwhile, make butterscotch sauce.

6 Serve warm puddings with warm butterscotch sauce.

butterscotch sauce Whisk butter and sugar in a medium saucepan, over medium heat, for 2 minutes or until melted and smooth. Add cream and salt; bring to a simmer; cook for 4 minutes or until thickened slightly.

tips You could also make the puddings in a texas muffin (¾-cup/180ml) pan. Serve the puddings warm with either greek-style yoghurt, double cream or vanilla ice-cream.

Watermelon, lime & BERRY CHEESECAKE JARS

PREP TIME 15 MINUTES **SERVES** 4

200g (6½ ounces) gingernut biscuits

50g (1½ ounces) butter

1 lime (90g)

250g (8 ounces) mascarpone cheese

250g (8 ounces) cream cheese

⅓ cup (55g) icing (confectioners') sugar

125g (4 ounces) raspberries

2 teaspoons icing (confectioners') sugar, extra

125g (4 ounces) seedless watermelon, diced into 1cm (½-inch) pieces

1 tablespoon finely shredded fresh mint

1 Pulse biscuits in a food processor until chopped finely. Add butter; pulse until just combined. Divide biscuit mixture into the bases of four 1½-cup (375ml) jars.

2 Finely grate rind of the lime then juice; you will need 2 tablespoons juice. Process lime rind and juice, cheeses and sifted icing sugar until smooth. Divide cheese mixture into jars; tap gently on a work surface to level mixture.

3 Place raspberries and extra icing sugar in a bowl. Using the back of a fork, lightly crush the berries, stirring until sugar dissolves. Stir in watermelon.

4 Divide watermelon mixture between jars; top with mint to serve.

CHOOSE A YELLOW-FLESHED PINEAPPLE, SUCH AS BETHONGA, FOR THE BEST FLAVOUR. YOU COULD ALSO USE MANGO CHEEKS CUT FROM FOUR MANGOES INSTEAD OF THE PINEAPPLE. DRIZZLE WITH PASSIONFRUIT PULP, IF YOU LIKE.

Mint syrup with GRILLED PINEAPPLE

PREP & COOK TIME 30 MINUTES SERVES 8

½ cup (110g) caster (superfine) sugar

½ cup (125ml) water

1½ cups firmly packed fresh round-leaf mint leaves

1 cup (50g) coconut flakes

1 medium yellow-fleshed pineapple (1.25kg), cut crossways into 1.5cm (¾-inch) thick slices

1 litre (4 cups) vanilla or passionfruit frozen yoghurt

¼ cup small fresh round-leaf mint leaves, extra

1 Preheat oven to 180°C/350°F.

2 Stir sugar and the water in a small saucepan, over medium heat, for 4 minutes or until sugar dissolves and syrup reduces slightly. Transfer to a small stainless steel bowl; freeze for 15 minutes to chill rapidly.

3 Meanwhile, place mint in a heatproof bowl, cover with boiling water; stand for 10 seconds. Drain, refresh under cold running water; squeeze to remove excess water.

4 Place coconut on an oven tray; bake, shaking the tray occasionally, for 3 minutes or until golden.

5 Preheat a large grill plate (or grill or barbecue) over medium-high heat. Cook pineapple, in two batches, for 2 minutes each side or until golden.

6 Process blanched mint and sugar syrup until finely chopped.

7 Divide grilled pineapple among plates; top with frozen yoghurt, drizzle with syrup. Serve sprinkled with coconut and extra mint.

Jam and peach DONUT PUDDINGS

PREP & COOK TIME 35 MINUTES SERVES 4

One of the joys of summer is peaches. This is a great dessert when stone fruit are in season, abundant and cheap! Nectarines could also be used, although they are a little more fragile than peaches.

2 eggs

⅔ cup (160ml) milk

⅔ cup (160ml) pouring cream

1 tablespoon caster (superfine) sugar

1 teaspoon vanilla bean paste or extract

4 jam donuts, halved crosswise (see tip)

2 yellow peaches, each cut into 8 thin wedges

1 Preheat oven to 180°C/350°F. Grease four 1-cup (250ml) ramekins.

2 Whisk eggs, milk, cream, sugar and vanilla in a medium bowl until combined.

3 Place 2 donut halves into each ramekin. Divide peaches into ramekins, pour egg mixture over top; stand for 5 minutes for mixture to soak into donuts slightly.

4 Place ramekins in a large roasting pan. Add enough boiling water to the pan to reach halfway up the side of ramekins. Bake puddings in oven for 25 minutes or until just set.

5 Dust puddings with sifted icing sugar to serve.

tip You could also use 8 mini jam ball donuts (220g).

Cheap EAT

Little cinnamon BANANA TARTE TATINS

75g (2½ ounces) butter

⅓ cup (75g) caster (superfine) sugar

½ teaspoon ground cinnamon

2 small firm bananas (260g), halved lengthways

2 sheets puff pastry

1 Preheat oven to 200°C/400°F.

2 Place butter, sugar and cinnamon in a large flameproof roasting pan over medium heat on the stove top, stir until butter is melted and mixture is combined and caramelised. Turn off the heat.

3 Meanwhile, place two banana halves, cut-side down, onto a pastry sheet. Trim pastry around bananas, following the shape, leaving a 1.5cm (¾-inch) border around each banana. Wrap pastry around curved banana halves. Repeat with remaining banana halves and pastry sheets.

4 Carefully place banana halves, cut-side down into the caramel mixture. Transfer to oven, bake for 20 minutes or until pastry is golden and cooked through. Stand for 5 minutes before carefully inverting tatins onto plates.

tip Serve dusted with icing sugar and ice cream.

Cherry & orange topped
CHOCOLATE MOUSSE

CHOCOLATE MOUSSE

PREP & COOK TIME 15 MINUTES (& STANDING) **SERVES** 4

200g (6½ ounces) dark (70% cocoa) chocolate

½ cup (100g) virgin coconut oil

300ml thickened (heavy) cream

1½ tablespoons icing (confectioners') sugar

½ cup (75g) fresh cherries

½ teaspoon finely grated orange rind

1 Break chocolate into pieces; place chocolate in a small heatproof bowl over a small saucepan of gently simmering water (don't allow water to touch bowl); stir until just melted. Add coconut oil; stir until just melted. Remove bowl from pan; stand until cooled to room temperature.

2 Meanwhile, beat cream and sifted icing sugar in a small bowl with an electric mixer until stiff peaks form.

3 Fold cream mixture into chocolate mixture, using a large metal spoon, just until combined.

4 Divide mixture into 1-cup (250ml) glasses or bowls. Refrigerate for 10 minutes only, before serving.

5 Top mousse with cherries and orange rind to serve.

tip Serve sprinkled with shaved chocolate.

CRUMBLE MIXTURE CAN BE MADE A DAY AHEAD; STORE IN AN AIRTIGHT CONTAINER. YOU CAN ALSO SERVE IT AS A TOPPING FOR OTHER DESSERTS, SUCH AS THE CHOCOLATE MOUSSE ON PAGE 224.

Spiced rhubarb and STRAWBERRY CRUMBLES

PREP & COOK TIME 25 MINUTES (& COOLING) SERVES 4

¼ cup (60ml) maple syrup

100g (3 ounces) shortbread, chopped coarsely

110g (3½ ounces) macadamia halves

1 bunch rhubarb (400g), trimmed, cut into 4cm (1½-inch) pieces

250g (8 ounces) strawberries, quartered

1 teaspoon vanilla extract

¼ cup (55g) caster (superfine) sugar

1 teaspoon ground ginger

½ teaspoon ground cinnamon

1 Preheat oven to 200°C/400°F. Grease and line an oven tray with baking paper.

2 Combine maple syrup, shortbread and macadamias in a medium bowl; spread out on oven tray. Bake, in oven, for 4 minutes; stir, then bake a further 4 minutes or until golden. Cool.

3 Meanwhile, place fruit, extract, sugar and spices in a medium saucepan over medium heat; cook stirring, for 3 minutes or until juices run from fruit. Cook, stirring occasionally, for a further 5 minutes or until rhubarb has softened but still holds its shape.

4 Divide fruit mixture among four small bowls; top with crumble mixture to serve.

Lemon honey & coconut
DELICIOUS PUDDINGS

PREP & COOK TIME 35 MINUTES SERVES 6

125g (4 ounces) butter, chopped

2 tablespoons honey

2 teaspoons finely grated lemon rind

1 cup (220g) caster (superfine) sugar

3 eggs, separated

½ cup (75g) self-raising flour

⅓ cup (80ml) lemon juice

1¾ cups (430ml) milk

2 tablespoons shredded coconut

1 teaspoon ground cardamom

¾ cup (160ml) double (thick) cream

1½ tablespoons icing (confectioners') sugar

2 teaspoons honey, extra

¼ cup (35g) coarsely chopped pistachios

1 Preheat oven to 180°C/350°F. Grease six 1-cup (250ml) ovenproof dishes.

2 Place butter and honey in a large saucepan; stir over low heat until just melted and mixture is combined. Stir in rind, caster sugar and yolks, then sifted flour and juice. Gradually stir in milk, coconut and cardamom; the mixture should be smooth and runny.

3 Whisk egg whites in a small bowl with an electric mixer until soft peaks form; fold into lemon mixture, in two batches.

4 Place ovenproof dishes in a large baking dish; divide lemon mixture into dishes. Add enough boiling water to baking dish to come halfway up sides of ovenproof dishes. Bake puddings for 25 minutes or until top is firm to touch.

5 Meanwhile, whisk cream and extra honey in a small bowl until soft peaks form.

6 Serve hot puddings immediately, dusted with sifted icing sugar, topped with spoonfuls of honey cream, and sprinkled with nuts.

Cheap
EAT

Meringue clouds
WITH MIXED BERRIES

PREP & COOK TIME 15 MINUTES   SERVES 6

3 egg whites

½ cup (110g) caster (superfine) sugar

1½ cups ready-made thick dairy custard

½ cup (125ml) thickened (heavy) cream

½ teaspoon vanilla bean paste

500g (1 pound) mixed fresh berries

1 tablespoon icing (confectioners') sugar, to dust

1 Beat egg whites in a medium bowl with an electric mixer until firm peaks form. Gradually add caster sugar. Divide mixture into 6 x 1-cup (250ml) microwave-safe teacups or ramekins.

2 Microwave on MEDIUM (80%) power for 1¾ minutes or until firm to the touch. (Meringue will soufflé, then sink).

3 Meanwhile, stir custard, cream and vanilla in a medium jug. Pour custard mixture among six small wide glasses. Divide half the berries into glasses. Slide meringue clouds onto berries, then top with remaining berries. Dust with sifted icing sugar before serving, if you like.

Chocolate and DULCE DE LECHE PUDDINGS

PREP & COOK TIME 50 MINUTES   SERVES 4

⅓ cup (120g) dulce de leche

¾ cup (165g) caster (superfine) sugar

100g (3 ounces) butter, melted, cooled

⅔ cup (100g) self-raising flour

2 tablespoons ground almonds

⅓ cup (35g) dutch-processed cocoa

⅓ cup (80ml) milk

2 eggs

1 teaspoon vanilla extract

50g (1½ ounces) dark (semi-sweet) chocolate, chopped finely

½ cup (110g) firmly packed brown sugar

1 cup (250ml) boiling water

1½ teaspoons dutch-processed cocoa, extra

4 small scoops vanilla ice-cream

1 Preheat oven to 200°C/400°F. Grease four 1⅓-cup (330ml) ovenproof dishes; place on a baking-paper-lined oven tray.

2 Spoon 1 tablespoon of the dulce de leche into the base of each dish.

3 Process caster sugar, butter, sifted flour, ground almonds, 2 tablespoons of the sifted cocoa, milk, eggs and extract until smooth. Transfer mixture to a large bowl; stir in chocolate. Spoon mixture evenly into dishes.

4 Combine brown sugar and remaining cocoa into a small bowl; sprinkle sugar mixture evenly over puddings. Pour the boiling water into a small jug. Holding the back of a spoon over each pudding, carefully pour ¼ cup boiling water over the surface of each pudding to wet the sugar mixture completely.

5 Bake puddings for 25 minutes or until the top is cake-like and firm to the touch. Dust with extra sifted cocoa. Serve immediately topped with ice-cream, and accompany with extra dulce de leche, if you like.

tip Dulce de leche is a caramel spread originating in South America. It is made by simmering sweetened milk until thick and caramelised. It is available in jars from delis. You can substitute Caramel Top 'n' Fill from supermarkets.

Glossary

ARTICHOKE HEARTS tender centre of the globe artichoke; purchased, in brine, canned or in glass jars.

BAMBOO SHOOTS the tender shoots of bamboo plants, available in cans; must be rinsed and drained before use.

BASIL an aromatic herb; there are many types, but the most commonly used is sweet, or common, basil.

thai basil, also known as horapa, has a sweet licorice flavour; it is available from Asian grocery stores and most major supermarkets.

BEANS

butter also known as lima beans; large, flat, kidney-shaped bean, off-white in colour, with a mealy texture and mild taste.

cannellini a small white bean similar in appearance and flavour to other white beans (great northern, navy or haricot), all of which can be substituted for the other. Available dried or canned.

snake long (about 40cm/16 inches), thin, round, fresh green beans, Asian in origin, with a taste similar to green or french beans. Are also known as yard-long beans because of their (pre-metric) length.

sprouts also known as bean shoots; tender new growths of assorted beans and seeds germinated for consumption.

white see cannellini beans.

BREADCRUMBS

packaged fine-textured, crunchy, purchased white breadcrumbs.

panko also known as japanese breadcrumbs. They are available in two types: larger pieces and fine crumbs. Both have a lighter texture than Western-style breadcrumbs. They are available from Asian grocery stores and larger supermarkets, and unless you make rather coarse breadcrumbs from white bread that's either quite stale or gently toasted, nothing is an adequate substitute. Have a crunchy texture with a delicate, pale golden colour.

stale one- or two-day-old bread made into crumbs by blending or processing.

BUK CHOY also known as buk choy, pak choi, chinese white cabbage or chinese chard; has a fresh, mild mustard taste. Use both stems and leaves. Baby buk choy, also known as pak kat farang or shanghai buk choy, is smaller and more tender than buk choy.

BUTTER use salted or unsalted (sweet) butter; 125g is equal to one stick of butter (4 ounces).

CAPERS grey-green buds of a warm climate shrub (usually Mediterranean); sold dried and salted or pickled in a vinegar brine. Baby capers are very small and have a fuller flavour. Rinse well before using.

CHEESE

blue these mould-treated cheeses are mottled with blue veining. Varieties include firm and crumbly stilton types to mild, creamy brie-like cheeses.

cream known as philadelphia or philly; a soft, cows'-milk cheese sold at supermarkets. Also available as a spreadable light cream cheese – a blend of cottage and cream cheeses.

fetta, danish (also danish white fetta) this type of fetta is a smooth and creamy variation of the more traditional fetta cheeses. The cheese is popular for its ability to be cubed and sliced without crumbling, and tossed into salads. Danish fetta has a very different taste to traditional fetta cheese. It has a milder taste, which makes it popular as an ingredient in baking.

fetta, persian a soft, creamy fetta marinated in a blend of olive oil, garlic, herbs and spices. Available from most larger supermarkets.

goat's made from goat's milk, has an earthy, strong taste; available in both soft and firm textures, in various shapes and sizes, and sometimes rolled in ash or herbs.

gorgonzola a creamy blue cheese having a mild, sweet taste.

gruyère a Swiss cheese with small holes and a nutty, slightly salty, flavour.

haloumi a firm, cream-coloured sheep-milk cheese matured in brine; haloumi can be grilled or fried, briefly, without breaking down. Should be eaten while still warm as it becomes tough and rubbery on cooling.

mascarpone a cultured cream product made in much the same way as yoghurt. Is whitish to creamy yellow in colour, with a soft, creamy texture and a rich, sweet, slightly acidic, taste.

pizza a blend of grated mozzarella, cheddar and parmesan cheeses.

CHILLI generally, the smaller the chilli, the hotter it is. Use rubber gloves when seeding and chopping fresh chillies as they can burn your skin. Removing seeds and membranes lessens the heat level.

cayenne pepper a long, thin-fleshed, extremely hot red chilli usually sold dried and ground.

long available both fresh and dried; a generic term used for any moderately hot, long (6cm-8cm), thin chilli.

red thai a small, hot, bright red chilli.

CHINESE BARBECUED PORK also called char siew. Has a sweet-sticky coating made from soy sauce, sherry, five-spice powder and hoisin sauce. Available from Asian food stores.

CHINESE COOKING WINE also known as shaoxing or chinese rice wine; made from fermented rice, wheat, sugar and salt with a 13.5 per cent alcohol content. Inexpensive and found in Asian food shops; if you can't find it, replace it with mirin or sherry.

CHORIZO a sausage of Spanish origin; made of coarsely ground pork and highly seasoned with garlic and chilli. They are deeply smoked, very spicy, and are available dry-cured or raw (which needs cooking).

CORIANDER also known as pak chee, cilantro or chinese parsley; a bright-green leafy herb with a pungent flavour. Both stems and roots of coriander are also used in cooking; wash well before using. Also available ground or as seeds; these should not be substituted for fresh coriander as the tastes are completely different.

COS LETTUCE also known as romaine.

COUSCOUS a fine, grain-like cereal product made from semolina.

CREAM we use fresh cream, also known as pure, pouring and single cream, unless otherwise stated.

CUMIN also known as zeera or comino; has a spicy, nutty flavour.

CURRY

curry powder a blend of ground spices used for convenience. Choose mild or hot to suit your taste.

green paste the hottest of the traditional pastes; contains chilli, garlic, onion, salt, lemon grass, spices and galangal.

tandoori paste a highly-seasoned classic East-Indian marinade flavoured with garlic, tamarind, ginger, coriander, chilli and other spices, and used to give foods the authentic red-orange tint of tandoor oven cooking.

tikka paste a medium-mild paste of chilli, coriander, cumin, lentil flour, garlic, ginger, turmeric, fennel, cloves, cinnamon and cardamom.

tom yum paste a Thai-style paste with a hot, spicy and sour flavour. Containing lemon grass, red chilli, sugar, onion, anchovy, galangal, kaffir lime and paprika. It is used to make the traditional spicy sour prawn soup known as tom yum goong.

DUKKAH is an Egyptian spice blend made with roasted nuts and aromatic spices. It is available from Middle-Eastern food stores, specialty spice stores and some supermarkets.

EGGPLANT also known as aubergine.

FENNEL also known as finocchio or anise; a white to very pale green-white, firm, crisp, roundish vegetable about 8-12cm in diameter. The bulb has a slightly sweet, anise flavour but the leaves have a much stronger taste. Also the name of dried seeds having a licorice flavour.

FISH FILLETS, FIRM WHITE blue eye, bream, flathead, swordfish, ling, whiting, jewfish, snapper or sea perch are all good choices. Check for small pieces of bone and use tweezers to remove them.

FIVE-SPICE POWDER also known as chinese five-spice; a fragrant mixture of cinnamon, cloves, star anise, sichuan pepper and fennel.

FLOUR

plain a general all-purpose wheat flour.

self-raising plain flour sifted with baking powder in the proportion of 1 cup flour to 2 teaspoons baking powder.

GALANGAL a rhizome with a hot ginger-citrusy flavour; used similarly to ginger and garlic as a seasoning or an ingredient.

KAFFIR LIME LEAVES also known as bai magrood. Aromatic leaves of a citrus tree; two glossy dark green leaves joined end to end, forming a rounded hourglass shape. A strip of fresh lime peel may be substituted for each kaffir lime leaf.

KECAP MANIS see sauces, soy.

KUMARA the Polynesian name of an orange-fleshed sweet potato often confused with yam.

LEBANESE CUCUMBER short, slender and thin-skinned. Probably the most popular variety because of its tender, edible skin, tiny, yielding seeds and sweet, fresh flavoursome taste.

LEMON GRASS a tall, clumping, lemon-smelling and -tasting, sharp-edged grass; the white part of the stem is used, finely chopped, in cooking.

LENTILS (red, brown, yellow) dried pulses often identified by and named after their colour; also known as dhal.

MAYONNAISE we use whole-egg mayonnaise in our recipes.

MESCLUN a salad mix or gourmet salad mix with a mixture of assorted young lettuce and other green leaves, including baby

MINCE also known as ground meat.

MIRIN a Japanese champagne-coloured cooking wine; made of glutinous rice and alcohol and used expressly for cooking. Should not be confused with sake.

MUSHROOMS

enoki have clumps of long, spaghetti-like stems with tiny, snowy white caps.

flat large, flat mushrooms with a rich earthy flavour. They are sometimes misnamed field mushrooms, which are wild mushrooms.

oyster also known as abalone; grey-white mushroom shaped like a fan. Prized for their smooth texture and subtle, oyster-like flavour.

shiitake when fresh are also known as chinese black, forest or golden oak mushrooms; although cultivated, they are large and meaty and have the earthiness and taste of wild mushrooms. When dried, they are known as donko or dried chinese mushrooms; rehydrate before use.

swiss brown also known as cremini or roman mushrooms; are light brown mushrooms with a full-bodied flavour.

MUSTARD SEEDS are available in black, brown or yellow varieties. Available from major supermarkets and health-food shops.

NOODLES

bean thread vermicelli made from mung bean flour. Fine, delicate noodles also known as wun sen, cellophane or glass noodles (because they are transparent when cooked). Available dried in various-sized bundles. Must be soaked to soften before use.

dried rice stick see rice vermicelli, dried (below).

egg, fresh also known as ba mee or yellow noodles. Made from wheat flour and eggs. Range in size from very fine strands to wide, thick spaghetti-like pieces as thick as a shoelace.

hokkien also known as stir-fry noodles; fresh wheat noodles resembling thick, yellow-brown spaghetti needing no pre-cooking.

ramen, fresh comes in various shapes and lengths. They may be fat, thin or even ribbon-like, as well as straight or wrinkled. While more often sold dried, fresh ramen is available from some Asian food stores. Substitute with reconstituted dried noodles.

rice vermicelli, dried very fine noodles made from rice flour and water, vermicelli is often compressed into blocks and dried. Before using, soak in boiling water until tender.

soba a thin spaghetti-like pale brown noodle from Japan; made from buckwheat and varying proportions of wheat flour.

ONIONS

green also known as scallion or, incorrectly, shallot; an immature onion picked before the bulb has formed. Has a long, bright-green edible stalk.

red also known as spanish, red spanish or bermuda onion; a sweet-flavoured, large, purple-red onion.

shallots also called french shallots, golden shallots or eschalots; small, brown-skinned, elongated members of the onion family.

spring have small white bulbs and long, narrow, green-leafed tops.

PAK CHOY similar to baby buk choy except the stem is a very pale

PAPRIKA ground, dried, sweet red capsicum (bell pepper); there are many types available, including sweet, hot, mild and smoked.

PARSLEY, FLAT-LEAF also known as continental or italian parsley.

PEPPERCORNS, SICHUAN also known as chinese pepper. Small, red-brown aromatic seeds resembling black peppercorns; they have a peppery-lemon flavour.

PITTA also known as lebanese bread.

PIZZA BASES pre-packaged for home-made pizzas. They come in a variety of sizes (snack or family) and thicknesses (thin and crispy or thick).

POLENTA also known as cornmeal; a flour-like cereal made of ground corn (maize). Also the name of the dish made from it.

PRAWN also known as shrimp.

PRESERVED LEMON RIND a North African specialty; lemons are quartered and preserved in salt and lemon juice or water. To use, remove and discard pulp, squeeze juice from rind, rinse rind well; slice thinly. Once opened, store under refrigeration.

PROSCIUTTO unsmoked italian ham; salted, air-cured and aged.

RICE

basmati a white, fragrant long-grained rice. Wash several times before cooking.

jasmine fragrant long-grained rice; white rice can be substituted, but will not taste the same.

RIGATONI a form of tube-shaped pasta. it is larger than penne and is usually ridged, the end doesn't terminate at an angle, like penne does.

ROCKET also known as arugula, rugula and rucola; a peppery-tasting green leaf that can be used similarly to baby spinach leaves. Baby rocket leaves are both smaller and less peppery.

SAMBAL OELEK (also ulek or olek) Indonesian in origin; a salty paste made from ground chillies and vinegar.

SAUCES

black bean a Chinese sauce made from fermented soya beans, spices, water and wheat flour.

char siu a Chinese barbecue sauce made from sugar, water, salt, fermented soya bean paste, honey, soy sauce, malt syrup and spices. It can be found at most supermarkets.

fish also called nam pla or nuoc nam; made from pulverised salted fermented fish, most often anchovies. Has a pungent smell and strong taste, so use sparingly.

hoisin a thick, sweet and spicy Chinese sauce made from salted fermented soya beans, onions and garlic.

oyster Asian in origin, this rich, brown sauce is made from oysters and their brine, cooked with salt and soy sauce, and thickened with starches.

plum a thick, sweet and sour dipping sauce made from plums, vinegar, sugar, chillies and spices.

soy made from fermented soya beans. Several variations are available in most supermarkets and Asian food stores.

dark soy deep brown, almost black in colour; rich, with a thicker consistency than other types. Pungent but not that salty.

japanese soy an all-purpose low-sodium soy sauce made with more wheat content than its Chinese counterparts. It is the best table soy and the one to choose if you only want one type.

kecap manis (ketjap manis); a thick soy sauce with added sugar and spices. The sweetness is derived from the addition of molasses or palm sugar.

light soy a fairly thin, pale but salty tasting sauce; used in dishes in which the natural colour of the ingredients is to be maintained. Do not confuse with salt-reduced or low-sodium soy sauces.

sweet chilli a mild sauce made from red chillies, sugar, garlic and vinegar.

SILVER BEET also known as swiss chard; mistakenly called spinach.

SNOW PEAS also called mange tout (eat all). Snow pea tendrils, the growing shoots of the plant, are also available at greengrocers. Snow pea sprouts are the tender new growths of snow peas.

SPINACH also known as english spinach and, incorrectly, silver beet.

SUGAR

brown very soft, finely granulated sugar retaining molasses for its characteristic colour and flavour.

caster also known as superfine or finely granulated table sugar.

palm also known as nam tan pip, jaggery, jawa or gula melaka; made from the sap of the sugar palm tree. Light brown to black in colour and usually sold in rock-hard cakes. Substitute with brown sugar if unavailable.

white coarsely granulated table sugar, also known as crystal sugar.

SUGAR SNAP PEAS also known as honey snap peas; fresh small peas that can be eaten whole, pod and all, similarly to snow peas.

SUMAC a purple-red, astringent spice ground from berries growing on shrubs flourishing wild around the Mediterranean; adds a tart, lemony flavour to food. Available from major supermarkets.

TAHINI a rich, sesame-seed paste.

TURMERIC related to ginger; adds a golden-yellow colour to food.

VINEGAR

balsamic originally from Modena, Italy, there are now many balsamic vinegars on the market ranging in pungency and quality depending on how long they have been aged. Is a deep rich brown colour and has a sweet and sour flavour. Quality can be determined up to a point by price; use the most expensive sparingly.

red wine based on fermented red wine.

rice a colourless vinegar made from fermented rice, sugar and salt. Also known as seasoned rice vinegar.

white made from spirit of cane sugar.

white wine made from white wine.

VIETNAMESE MINT not a mint at all, but a pungent and peppery narrow-leafed member of the buckwheat family.

WHITE MISO (SHIRO) Japan's famous bean paste made from fermented soya beans and rice, rye or barley. It varies in colour, texture and saltiness. Available from supermarkets.

WOMBOK also known as napa, peking or chinese cabbage or petsai. Elongated in shape with pale green, crinkly leaves.

Conversion chart

Measures

One Australian metric measuring cup holds approximately 250ml; one Australian metric tablespoon holds 20ml; one Australian metric teaspoon holds 5ml.

The difference between one country's measuring cups and another's is within a two- or three-teaspoon variance, and will not affect your cooking results.
North America, New Zealand and the United Kingdom use a 15ml tablespoon.

All cup and spoon measurements are level. The most accurate way of measuring dry ingredients is to weigh them. When measuring liquids, use a clear glass or plastic jug with the metric markings.

The imperial measurements used in these recipes are approximate only. Measurements for cake pans are approximate only. Using same-shaped cake pans of a similar size should not affect the outcome of your baking. We measure the inside top of the cake pan to determine sizes.

We use large eggs with an average weight of 60g.

Dry measures

METRIC	IMPERIAL
15G	½OZ
30G	1OZ
60G	2OZ
90G	3OZ
125G	4OZ (¼LB)
155G	5OZ
185G	6OZ
220G	7OZ
250G	8OZ (½LB)
280G	9OZ
315G	10OZ
345G	11OZ
375G	12OZ (¾LB)
410G	13OZ
440G	14OZ
470G	15OZ
500G	16OZ (1LB)
750G	24OZ (1½LB)
1KG	32OZ (2LB)

Liquid measures

METRIC	IMPERIAL
30ML	1 FLUID OZ
60ML	2 FLUID OZ
100ML	3 FLUID OZ
125ML	4 FLUID OZ
150ML	5 FLUID OZ
190ML	6 FLUID OZ
250ML	8 FLUID OZ
300ML	10 FLUID OZ
500ML	16 FLUID OZ
600ML	20 FLUID OZ
1000ML (1 LITRE)	1¾ PINTS

Length measures

METRIC	IMPERIAL
3MM	⅛IN
6MM	¼IN
1CM	½IN
2CM	¾IN
2.5CM	1IN
5CM	2IN
6CM	2½IN
8CM	3IN
10CM	4IN
13CM	5IN
15CM	6IN
18CM	7IN
20CM	8IN
22CM	9IN
25CM	10IN
28CM	11IN
30CM	12IN (1FT)

Oven temperatures

The oven temperatures in this book are for conventional ovens; if you have a fan-forced oven, decrease the temperature by 10-20 degrees.

	°C (CELSIUS)	°F (FAHRENHEIT)
VERY SLOW	120	250
SLOW	150	300
MODERATELY SLOW	160	325
MODERATE	180	350
MODERATELY HOT	200	400
HOT	220	425
VERY HOT	240	475

Index